TERMINAL

Velocity

**Changing your attitude towards
health, finances and life after diagnosis**

MICHAEL ROMEO

Published by Share Your Story
Share Your Story
PO BOX 5447
Alexandra Hills QLD 4161
Printed by Ingram Sparks

First published in Australia 2020
This edition published 2020
Copyright © Michael Romeo 2020
Cover design, typesetting: WorkingType (www.workingtype.com.au)
Photograph supplied by Photography by Marzena

Romeo, Michael
Terminal Velocity: Managing your Money and Mindset after Diagnosis
ISBN Paperback 9780648773207
ISBN Ebook 9780648773214
pp172

This book is dedicated to
Cristine and Giulia

Contents

Preface

Up until January 2019, I was a healthy 35-year-old. I spent my youth keeping in shape, training, eating right and generally looking after myself. That all changed when I was diagnosed with Oesophageal Cancer. Now, I spend my days visiting various hospitals, having my arms poked and prodded with needles, trying different drugs and abusing my body in the hope that something might help cure me of this evil disease. Overnight my life was changed, and I started to see life from a totally new perspective. It is one that I hope can help others.

Through sharing my story and situation in regard to my health and finances, I hope that I can offer advice and perspective, especially when it comes to changing our attitudes and outlook on life.

From the beginning, we are governed by rules and are taught to listen to complete strangers who society hold in high regard, from medical professionals to financial institutions. We are taught to listen to these people with no questions asked and take whatever substance they prescribe. I mean, in the 20th century we have been to the moon and we are searching for life on other planets, yet we are still debating what is good for us to eat. As a human race we are faced with an obesity epidemic, and major health issues all round the world.

Here in Australia, from primary school we are all taught how to save money. We are encouraged by the big financial institutions to open our bank accounts and once a week bring in our little banking wallet with our pocket money earned from doing chores, washing dishes, cleaning up our room etc. I remember this well and was always excited to bring in my cash and watch it slowly grow. Unfortunately, my hard-earned cash did not grow as much as I hoped. I remember back in the early days, I would save my coins in my little money box at home and every now and then would empty this onto the carpet and sit there and count, seeing how much I managed to save from the weeks before. I would be excited to see how much I managed to save. Throughout life, I continued to save money, putting it aside in my separate bank account, trying to get ahead.

Growing up was not easy for me. My father passed away when I was very young and from that point on, my mother had to put on a brave face and pretty much overnight support a family of four on her own as my father didn't have any insurances in place. Mum was never one to sit around and cry over spilt milk, so without hesitation she was back to work, earning money to pay the bills as she had no other option. Her work ethic was very contagious and me and my siblings learnt to get by on whatever resources we had on hand. We never had the best things growing up but it made us respect where they come from, and appreciate the smaller things in life, being happy with what we have and not wanting the trendy or top of the range things every time something new came along.

I went through the public-school system and I finished Grade 12. I stayed at school mainly to play rugby league. My dream was to play for Australia and as I had some talent, found myself selected in representative teams. I remember telling teachers I did not have to worry about my schooling or education as I would be a famous footy player one day. This dream never came to fruition, partly due to a re-occurring shoulder injury which resulted in a shoulder reconstruction. I started working, completing my carpentry apprenticeship.

I decided to move to the UK to work and travel. In my time overseas, I worked hard, constantly working 60, 70, 80 hrs a week, but hey, I was moving up in the corporate world and got into project/construction management. I'm not complaining about working all those hours. At the time, things were good. I found myself in a well-paid job but still had no money left over at the end of the month. The bills just kept coming in. I would pay one off then the next one would come in. I budgeted each week to put money aside for these bills, but something always popped up in the meantime.

Once we finish school and enter the world of employment, things change and not always for the best. The unfortunate thing in the 20th century is that we are surrounded by advertisements, media and social media, enticing us to buy and consume items which we really don't need. I'm not saying we should not buy anything and live a minimalist lifestyle; however, we need to recognize what is good debt and what will hinder our financial success. For instance, we all look to buy the latest gadgets, have the biggest screen TV's, new cars every few years or upgrade to the newer model, let alone health insurances, rising electrical bills or university debit.

I met my wife and we saved as hard as we could for an average size wedding. We settled down and looked to buy a house. We were happy to start at the bottom and work our way up, have kids, pay for schooling etc. The list went on and on and never seemed to end.

The banks offered us a credit card, with unrealistic, unmanageable limits, but we didn't say no. We used them cautiously at first, then we got comfortable and all of a sudden, we had debts in the tens of thousands, asking ourselves how the hell did that happen?

Subconsciously, we had this fear of the credit card and looked at it with apprehension. It made us feel guilty to use it. In the end, my wife refused to have a line of credit and cut her credit cards up. The big financial institutions had us where they wanted us, in the mindset that we must go to work, exchange out time for money, be good little humans and pay our monthly mortgage / bills.

We budgeted and spent wisely, never missing a mortgage payment, but God forbid the day came and something happened to our situation with work, got laid off or injured and missed a payment or two. Do you think the banks would let us off or go easy on us? The answer is NO. They will get their money any way they can and even reposes your house if they need to. I know this firsthand, as it happened to my own family home. This was a stressful and difficult time, but one that could have been avoided.

We created this fear within our minds that the credit cards or line of credit was a bad tool, not really understanding how they could be used to our advantage. Does this sound familiar? I am here to tell you from my own personal experience that this is completely FALSE!

I am NOT a licensed attorney, accountant, financial advisor, broker or any other licensed individual. Therefore, I cannot provide any specific council, advise or instruction that would apply to specific individuals. This book is about my personal cancer diagnosis, prognosis and experience with a finance strategy and is intended to be general information only. I recommend you engage the services of professionals in making decisions that have a legal impact especially financial decision.

We need to realize that by staying in this mindset of trading our time for money, the banks will always have you in their back pocket and you will never be rid of the financial burden. We need to open our minds and look to change our attitude, before it's too late.

Chapter 1

How Quickly Things Can Change!

I was your average 35-year-old. Life was going along as usual; work, family, training, keeping fit and eating right. This is what we are taught and if we do all these things than we will be able to live a long and happy life. Right? Wrong!

I have always been a sporty, outdoors type of person and have been what I consider to be fit and healthy. After having a very mild case of reflux while on our family holiday in Italy, my wife insisted I have it looked at. I went to the doctors not expecting much, but boy, I was wrong.

When I was only four years old, my father passed away from a rare blood disease called Thrombotic Thrombocytopenic Purpura (TTP) which left my mother with four mouths to feed. To her credit, she did her best and us kids could not have asked for more. She worked hard and provided a decent life for us, and at the same time embedded the hard-working Australian attitude in all of us. Years later, Mum re-married and our stepfather, who was a great role model, showed me how to behave like a gentleman, take responsibility for my actions and most of all, to continue to work hard.

When I was nine years old, I began playing Rugby League and played up until the age of 24. I finished high school and went into the workforce. My first job was working as a labourer on building sites with my stepfather who encouraged me to start a carpentry apprenticeship. Because I was chasing my dream of playing in the NRL, I refused the offer. I was playing Rugby League at semi-professional level which involved training 4-6 days a week, and I was confident I would make the big time and be playing in the NRL before long, however this dream did not become my reality. I retired due to a recurring shoulder injury which required a shoulder reconstruction and I was left thinking, 'what now?'

When I was 20 years old, I finally started my carpentry apprenticeship which I completed in 2007, becoming a qualified carpenter at the age of 24. Throughout this time, I was living at home with my parents who were supportive of me but continued to instil a hard-working attitude. If I wanted something, I would have to earn it. One of my chores was to wash the dishes, and it became a running joke with my friends as they would be outside waiting in the car to go out for the night but I could not leave until the dishes were washed, dried and put away. Half the time they would come inside and help, just to get us out of there quicker. While living at home I was paying rent, which obviously went to the bills, however Mum would put aside $50 a week into a savings account for me and my sister. It took years of saving and I am very grateful to my mother for doing this, as it enabled my sister and I to buy our first house together 50/50.

I moved to London not long after finishing my carpentry apprenticeship. I wanted to challenge myself and stand on my own two feet, proving to myself that I could make it on my own. I had a few friends living over in London which made the move a little easier, but none the less daunting as I had never done anything like that before. I was sleeping (dossing as they call it in the UK) on couches, paying 5 pounds a night and literally living out of my suitcase for months.

I began working odd jobs here and there through labour hire companies, working all round London, dragging my tool box round behind me, sometimes through the snow to get to my job sites, even getting the A-Z (London Street Directory) out in the rain to navigate my way around the busy streets of London. It was difficult but at the same time it was exciting. The time spent in London was a great time and one I look back on now and really appreciate. It showed me how strong and independent I was and taught me to really chase what I wanted, without being influenced by my surroundings.

In the UK, Australian workers have a really good reputation as being hard working people and it was never hard to find work. I took pride in this and in turn I was earning my paycheck each week. I would enjoy travelling around Europe with friends throughout the summer, then return to work and save my pennies.

Whilst travelling in Italy, I met a girl, but it was when we arrived back in London that we started our relationship. We were both of the mindset that we must work hard to earn a living. My girlfriend was forging out her own career in the project logistics field and would regularly work late at the office, staying behind to ensure the deadlines were met. I would work away for extended periods and only return home for a brief stay before heading back off to work all around the UK, all to earn money to pay for our ever-increasing bills. We lived an average lifestyle, nothing fancy, meeting with friends to have dinner and a few beers every now and then. We would go travelling when we could, in between work commitments, which was a passion that we both shared.

I proposed to my now wife in 2012 and in Oct 2013, we tied the knot. We arranged a wedding in Sorrento, near Naples, as this was where we had met and was basically halfway for both our families and friends to fly in for the wedding as my wife is originally from Brazil. The wedding cost us around €25,000 (Euros) which we had to fund ourselves. We basically used all our savings, and then put the rest on credit cards and paid bills where we could afford. We would spend the next 3 to 5 years paying off our wedding.

We looked at entering the property market in London about six months after the wedding and all while still trying to pay off the wedding. With the ever-increasing talks of housing prices on the rise and we were worried how are we, the next generation, were never going to be able to afford a property if we didn't act now. We decided to go for it and take the risk. Luckily, we were able to take money from the equity in the property I bought with my sister a few years back in Australia which gave us the deposit.

We found a home on the outskirts of London and started carrying out some minor renovations. In the first two weeks after moving in, we found out my wife was pregnant. This was an exciting time, but also very scary as it would change everything in terms of our financial situation.

Our daughter was born, and life was good. I was still working crazy hours, but we were managing things. My wife accepted a temporary job offer over the Christmas period, finishing her maternity leave when our daughter was only six months old. When the temp role was complete, the company actually offered her a permanent position, with the option of relocating to Australia, which was hard to turn down. She accepted it and working full time again a month before our daughter turned one.

Prior to her taking up the new position, we had already spoken about moving back to Australia, but we were not in a strong enough financial position to do so. When we left the UK, we decided to keep the property, as a friend was happy to move in and rent it from us. However, the rent did not cover the mortgage and we had to transfer money back each month. We were hopeful of keeping this property as a long-term investment and possibly for our daughter if she ever decided to go travelling or study abroad.

We returned to Australia in May 2017, with the aim of settling down and buying our forever home and raising our daughter. Things were looking up. We both came back to Australia with jobs and my sister and I managed to sell our property here in Australia for double what we paid. This was a great stepping stone and three months after arriving back in Australia we made the purchase of our forever home in September 2017. It was a crazy idea but we just both fell in love with the property, which again put us under a lot of financial pressure and not to mention stress, but this was the home we were looking to grow old in. We thought it was worth the leap and risk as things were looking good.

How quickly that all changed!

After being back in Australia for one year and being in our new home, things were starting to become too much for us financially. We were constantly worrying about paying bills and having regular arguments about our financial situation. At the beginning of 2018, we decided to sell the property in the UK as we could simply not afford to pay our own mortgage and send money back to pay a second mortgage. This was a tough decision as we had put a lot of hard work into getting the property in the UK. It was where our daughter was born, so it had a very strong sentimental connection with us. We even named our dog after the street so our daughter would know her origin.

With all the pressure and stress we were under at this point in our lives, there was only one thing we could do and that was to just keep working and paying our debts, like the majority of the population, but things were not looking good. We had further talks about selling our own home at a loss and moving into a smaller property in a different area, because we knew we had overstretched ourselves.

It was while we were visiting my sister between Christmas and New Year's 2018-2019 that my wife came across a book called The Barefoot Investor by Scott Pape. She read a few pages and got really excited about the strategy. Even though we had well-paying jobs, at this point in our lives we were still were struggling with debt and there never seemed to be any money left over at the end of the month. It sounded like the best new year's resolution ever. We decided to apply the strategy from The Bare Foot Investor as soon as 2019 arrived.

We created new bank accounts (buckets) ready to start splitting our monies each month into these new buckets. We sat down for our weekly meetings, which were going great and made us feel like we were on top of things again. It was on one of our first meetings that we discovered that my life insurance was inadequate. It turned out I had the bare minimum through my superannuation fund which was a measly $245,000. Our total debts at this point where around $1.25 million. We scheduled our next meeting to finally sort our insurances out which we had through our super.

On the 23rd of January, the day before our scheduled meeting to fix our insurance, at 8.30pm, when my wife was putting our daughter to bed, I received a phone call from the doctor who broke the news that my recent Endoscopy had come back positive for a cancerous tumour in my Oesophagus.

I had been diagnosed with an aggressive form of Cancer (Oesophageal Adenocarcinoma at the Gastro-Oesophageal Junction or GOJ).

The next day, instead of organising my insurance, I was booked in for a CT/ PET Scan. My tumour was stage 2 out of 4, nodes was 1 out of 3, metastasis was 0 from 3. In my case, the cancer had already spread into a lymph node beside the tumour, which is the first signs of the metastatic involvement. If undetected, this cancer spreads to lungs, liver and stomach and can become terminal.

Overall, I was being told that this could be cured as it was still an early detection. From the outset, the doctors were all telling me that time was of the essence and I needed to act fast.

After the Australia Day long weekend, which may I say was the longest fucking weekend ever, I was booked in to see the surgeon who explained the detailed and difficult surgery which I needed to undergo for the tumour to be removed. This surgery was an Esophagectomy with gastric reconstruction by abdominal mobilisation and thoracotomy, which basically would involve removing as much of my stomach and Oesophagus as possible then joining them back together.

Thursday, I met the Oncologist and then Friday I was booked in to undergo a minor surgery to install a central intravenous line in my left arm, ready for my first chemotherapy on Monday the 4th of February. This was a whirlwind of a week. It felt like a month had passed in this short time.

My wife went from making travel arrangements for a work conference in London, to suddenly researching Adenocarcinoma at the Gastro-Oesophageal junction.

We had some difficult conversations throughout this week, like not knowing if I would get to see my daughter's 4th birthday in May, or my wife's birthday, our wedding anniversary in October, or even getting to Christmas! The unknown was the hardest thing to deal with and still is to this day.

To add to the stress of the diagnosis, the realization of leaving nothing but a massive debt for my wife and daughter to inherent sunk in and really hurt the most. One thing I have come to learn is that I am not the only one to have the incorrect attitude towards money, health and insurances. I spoke with many friends and family regarding this and explained the implications of not having prioritized my own personal health and insurance policies and now it's all too late for me to make any changes. We got sucked into the lifestyle of working hard for our money and pushing our health aside, always believing something like this would never happen to me. It's always someone we know. Well, when it happened to us, it really hit home, and the implications are irreversible and damaging. This is my biggest regret to date.

With the diagnosis and feelings of regret, not to mention disappointment within myself at my own stupidity, this was not the time to be lying down and admitting defeat to this horrible disease! I felt like something had to be done, something which I could take responsibility for, and the only thing I felt I could control at this point was my diet. My focus turned to my diet throughout four cycles of chemo and I made it my obsession to focus on what I was eating, to limit the bad processed foods which are so readily available these days. I was eating fresh fruit and vegetables, trying to manage my blood glucose levels and even went to the extent of sourcing a fully grass-fed cow from a friend, all in an attempt to rid this disease from my body by trying to cut down any unnecessary chemicals which we are all exposed to on a daily basis. Chemo took a toll on my body. It was not easy, and it was every bit as horrible as I imagined. All the usual side effects; nausea, tingling in the hands and feet, feeling like your internal organs are shaking constantly, hot and cold sweats, the list goes on!

Due to an infection to my central line after the third bout of chemo, I developed a 5cm blood clot in my left arm. I had to go onto blood thinning medication which I injected into my stomach morning and night. It was horrible to say the least and it also meant my surgery had to be pushed back another 6 weeks. It was through this period I was feeling like this was the beginning of the end. I was unable to play with my daughter. I would go from the lounge to the chair, play with her for five minutes and then need to lay back down. With each treatment, the side effects were amplified, and I was feeling worse and worse. By focusing on my diet, I was able to channel what little energy I had into something good and that made me feel like I was doing something right. My goal in between each treatment was to maintain my weight and each time I walked in to receive my treatment.

I would look at it like a boxer being weighed in for the fight of my life. I am happy to say I managed to go through chemo and actually put on .7kgs! This was a little win for me.

PIC OF LAST CHEMO IN HOSPITAL — the final weigh in. I managed to put on .7kgs, I was happy with this result as I had managed to maintain my weight and accomplish my goal.

It was on Anzac Day 2019, one week before my operation, that I managed to drag myself out of the house and go with my wife, daughter and a friend to the dawn service to pay my respects to our fallen soldiers. I thought to myself this could possibly be the last time I would get to do this. It was only by chance, sitting and chatting afterwards with a friend over a beer, that we briefly spoke of financial pressures and debt. My friend spoke about what is known as the 'velocity' banking strategy which is more known in the USA and Canada. Here in Australia, we only have a few banking tools such as re-draw facility and off set accounts which the banks provide, unlike the USA and Canada.

It got me interested and I wondered if this strategy could be implemented in Australia. I wondered if it was worthwhile looking further into it.

That same night, my wife was putting our daughter to bed and I started doing some more research. I was probably 20 minutes into a YouTube video, when I texted my wife.

'Babe, we gotta talk.'

She came down ten minutes later and said, 'Oh dear, what now?'

She watched the video with me in silence, and we knew then it was the best strategy for us, as the 'barefoot' strategy is a long-term strategy and for us, time was of the essence.

I started doing my own research.

There is the age old saying if it looks too good to be true then it probably is. I must admit I have looked into quite a few different investment strategies over the years to help our situation and I would speak with accountants and financial brokers, who all had valid reasons not to attempt these other strategies. We were always led back to just keep paying the mortgage. It's something we had to do and that was part of life. Due to my circumstances, I could no longer accept this as a final answer and if there was something else out there, I was going to find it to help my family in a last-ditch effort to ease our financial burden.

Just like my weight and diet, my focused turned to this strategy and over the coming week, I studied and carried out my own research. I went into the bank and spoke with the mortgage advisor (not giving away my intentions), who continually told me to take out more offset accounts or to lock in my mortgage at the lower rate. I spoke with a mortgage broker who told me to stay clear of this strategy, instead suggesting when we paid more off our home, we could just get an investment loan and buy a rental property.

I continued to research.

I read articles, spoke with an accountant who this time said it looks like a valid strategy and made sense. First time for everything, right?

I looked into the amortized v's simple interest and different lines of credit, sifting through the internet to find what I could on the pros and cons for this strategy. At first, I was unsure if this could be true, but the more I looked into this strategy and did the figures with my own home loan, I came to the realization that this could actually work for us.

After all the research I was left shocked, disgusted and angered to see just how much we are being robbed by the banks. For instance, on the fixed part of our home loan of $590,423, I calculated that for us to get to a point in the loan where we are paying more principal than interest, we would need to pay the bank a total of $330,107, consisting of $193,970 in interest and only knocking $136,169 off the principal. So why not use the banks own money to pay our debt? It sounded like a great payback plan!

My wife and I made the decision to move forward with this strategy. I went to the bank that same week, just before my surgery and applied for a $20,000 Line of Credit which we would put to good use.

By implementing this strategy, it made an instant change and one that really helped my wife and I realize that there was a light at the end of the debt tunnel and helped to take the focus off the cancer diagnosis. It gave us hope that we were on the right track to achieving the lifelong goal of paying off our mortgage. Even if I was to die early, it was something my wife could can carry on doing on her own and still benefit from the strategy, which again gave me comfort and also gave her the strength that she would be able to carry on doing what we set out to do.

My devastating prognosis

In June, four days after my 36th birthday, I returned to the surgeon for my six week post op follow up appointment and was expecting I would receive some good news, something like 'we got it early enough and have managed to cut out the tumours', meaning I would be cured.

The surgeon however, told me the result of my latest PET SCAN could 'not be worse' and 'I would die of oesophageal cancer'. The cancer had spread to the liver, stomach and neck in the short space of six weeks and the tumours in the liver were bigger than the original one in my Oesophagus. I was upgraded to stage 4 Oesophageal Cancer. There is no stage 5. It was terminal and at this point I was given 6-12 months to live.

So, for me, now more than ever, time was fast running out and potentially I would never achieve the lifelong dream of reaching financial freedom by paying off my home mortgage.

Terminal velocity was born.

Basically, I have done all the hard work and am now sharing our story in hope I can change peoples' attitude towards money, health and their priorities in life after my terminal diagnosis.

Out of this really shitty situation, we discovered a positive strategy which can make a big difference in a short period of time. The only thing that was stopping us was our attitude towards our money and how we were using the financial tools available to us. Since deciding to start the new strategy, it has been the main focus for me and my wife and it's exciting to see the possibilities, realising that we can actually be debt free in a very short period of time. But for me, I just need more time! There is now hope for my family and if I can do it, then others can as well.

Summary

→   Prioritize your health

→   Know your insurances

→   Work hard but with a purpose and a clear focus

→   Enjoy your money where you can and don't be happy to give it away because you think you have to.

Chapter 2

Realizing and Changing Our Attitude

Reasons not to attempt this strategy

During my research, the only foreseeable reason not to start this new banking strategy was simple.

DO NOT ATTEMPT THIS STRATEGY IF YOU HAVE A NEGATIVE CASHFLOW.

I spoke with many people during my journey and the most consistent response I got from people I spoke with, friends and family alike, was always 'we are not strict enough with our money', or 'you do it first and let me know if it works'.

Well, that is exactly what we have done.

We, as humans, are creatures of habit. We go to the same shopping centres because we like the way the shop feels and how its laid out, and we can find what we need every time. We go to the same holiday destination for 30 years, not changing as we know it's good and we like to stick to things we know. The old saying, 'if it aint broke, don't fix it', means we do things out of habit.

How many people tell you they like to get into a routine, wake at 6am to exercise, go to work, gym in the afternoon, home to cook dinner see the kids for an hour or so then off to bed and do it all again the very next day? Sounds robotic, right? This is exactly what we have become in the 20th century, robots. Going to work to pay for things like our 30-year mortgage.

Because of the pressures of life and the need to keep up with our demanding lifestyles, convenience is becoming an important part of life. We are buying readymade meals for breakfast, lunch and dinner and grabbing a coffee on the way to work as we didn't have time to sit down with the family to have breakfast. The same goes with our finances. Why do you think we are encouraged to use our cards and not pay with cash anymore? Because it's more convenient, saves time and makes it easy for us to spend on the go. We simply think that changing what we are doing is just too time consuming and there is not worthwhile making those changes, as there is no way to beat the system.

I would like to challenge people's attitude and to be open minded to a different way of thinking, realising that making a few changes does not take much time at all, is not that difficult and can save you thousands in the process.

Basically, we set aside a small amount of time after dinner (or whatever works for you) and we simply set up basic principles and re-structured our finances to benefit us. Once this was done, it simply worked on its own and all we had to do was monitor our situation.

Changing Our Attitude

When it comes to money and finances, we are all afraid of making changes as we think we may not be educated enough, therefore we put our trust in the large financial institutions, or mortgage brokers who are lending us money. We trust the financial institutions to have our best interests at heart. They are regulated and therefore they would not be able to take advantage of the little guy, right? I'm not saying what they are doing is illegal, as its not, it's simply we are not educated correctly in the tools they have on offer as we have never been taught anything different. Everything we know about the banks and their lending tools are what they have been teaching us since we started school.

They are teaching us what they want us to know.

Once we educated ourselves on what other options

were out there, we could change our way of thinking and attitude to make a change that would benefit us in a more positive way.

Most of us have an emotional connection with money, which makes it more difficult to make changes with our finance. According to figures provided to The New Daily by the Treasury itself, the average wage in Australia is just over $62,000 a year and to earn the weekly wage, we must trade at least 38 hours a week. If we need to earn more, we need to work longer hours. What does this mean? It means we must make sacrifices in life, like missing our kids first day at school. We work the weekends and miss sporting and family events. Single parents struggle to make ends meet, just like my mother all those years ago, all to provide for their family, and for what? To give our hard-earned money to the big financial institutions in the way of interest payments. To earn that little bit more, we must sacrifice something in some area of our lives. So, suddenly, we see money as not the cash in our pocket, but the time spent earning it and all the little things that we are sacrificing along the way.

I was a prime example of this.

I was constantly working 80 to 90 hours a week shop fitting. The biggest week I worked was 127 hours, which included travelling to and from other job sites, working day and nights, getting minimal sleep in the van when possible, pushing my health and safety aside. To put this into perspective, there are only 168 hours in 7 days, and I worked 127 hours, leaving only 41 hours to sleep! This was definitely not healthy or safe to be working on a building site. I was living out of a hotel room, cooking my instant noodles in a filthy kettle jug, returning home to visit my wife once a month. I would arrive on a Friday evening and leave again Sunday morning. Looking back now, I was not only losing out on time bonding with my daughter, but also putting my health at risk. During the working week it was very difficult to eat right, missing out on sleep all whilst working with power tools, working at heights and navigating many different hazards on these building sites. Fatigue would set in towards the end of the week, which made driving home dangerous, nearly falling asleep at the wheel many times, but I was in the mindset that I was making an honest living and getting ahead in this rat race.

My wife was the same as me. She was forging a career in her field of work and was always working late to get the job done. There were many nights she would spend in the office and return home at 10, 11, 12 o'clock, only to get some rest and then wake early commute to work and do it all again. At one point, my wife was commuting 2.5 hours each way to get to work, adding an unpaid 15 hours a week to her already demanding schedule.

My older brother, at 43 years old, is another example of this mindset and attitude towards working, trading time for money and providing for the family. I'm not saying this is not a good mindset to be in, as I have always looked up to my brother and have admired his dedication to his family through his hard work. It's inspirational. My brother started working from the age of 15 and bought his first home at the age of 30 with his wife. Since then, he has worked even harder day and night pushing his health and safety aside as he has debts to pay and needs to provide for his family. My brother worked for a few years as an underground minor, mining for coal. He was hit by a coal tram, which is a very large piece of equipment and he is lucky to be alive. He did not have much time off work and actually returned back only four weeks after the incident out of fear of losing his job. He had pressure from the company to get back to work so it did not become a reportable incident due to time off work. He has since changed jobs, yet as a direct result from his injuries he finds himself struggling in pain some mornings to get out of bed and on a few occasions, he has not been able to at all. His back just seizes up, causing him excruciating pain. His new role is still physically demanding, working with concreting precast panels, starting at 4am and finishing anywhere from 3-5pm in the afternoon 5 to 6 days a week.

Since my diagnosis, I have spoken with my brother many times and I cannot stress to him enough that he may be driving himself to what could be an early grave. I am sure his wife and three kids would not like this to happen to their hard working, devoted father, all in an attempt to provide a get-by lifestyle for his family.

Ask yourselves the question; 'is working like a dog, putting your body through all this stress and pain really going to be worth it in the end if you are never really getting ahead?'

Working Smarter

Being told you have six months to live is very difficult to grasp if you are not in that situation and I get that, but it really does make you appreciate the things in life which we so easily take for granted because we are chasing what we think to be an honest living. I am not saying that we don't need to work hard, because we do, and through my cancer battle I have continued to work when I have been able. I have been blessed as the company I work for has continued to pay me through this difficult time and this would not usually be the case for many others in this position and myself and my family are forever grateful. What I am saying is that we need to work smarter, change our attitude and to make our money work for us instead of continuing to exchange our time for money.

The problem here is that there is only so much time we can trade to make our money, and what we make is limited because we can only earn more if our hourly rate or salary is increased. The simple equation 'Time = Money' makes it very difficult for the average person like me and my wife to ever truly get a head in life and eliminate the financial burden so many of us face on a daily basis.

After having re-assessed our situation following the cancer diagnosis, my wife and I now have a relative healthy cashflow per month. This is testament to our willingness to make sacrifices and hard work along the way. It has not been an easy road but one we can be proud of. For years, even with well paid jobs, we found ourselves struggling at the end of the month to make ends meet and pay our bills and to support our modest lifestyle.

Before we re-structured our finances, our original joint cashflow was around $4,000 per month but this increased to $6,500 after I received my terminal illness insurance money. In my case my death insurance was the minimum $245,000 which didn't cover our total debt of around $1.25m (Insurance cover should be relative to debt. Prioritize this before it's too late!) We put this directly onto the home loan, even though we had to pay the bank $6,000 to break from a fixed loan to a variable loan.

The key to knowing if this strategy would be beneficial to us was to firstly figure out if we had a positive or negative cashflow.

Negative Cashflow

Simply put, negative cashflow is if our total income is less than our total expenses then we have a negative cashflow.

For a visual see the below equation.

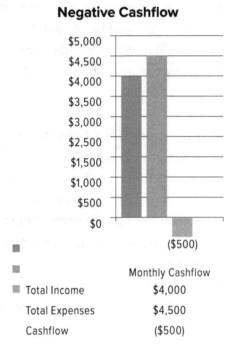

Negative Cashflow

	Monthly Cashflow
Total Income	$4,000
Total Expenses	$4,500
Cashflow	($500)

Graph 2.1
Negative cash flow which would not
be sustainable in the long run

Example Total Income $4000pcm – All expenses pcm $4500 = cashflow -$500

This meant that at the end of every month, we were spending more than what was coming in. Using things like the dreaded credit card to pay for a bill to buy us more time and simply just keeping our head above water was not getting us anywhere. This was not a sustainable way to live. If this is you then now more than ever something needs to change, and you need to break free. It will be a difficult road. You will need to assess what is necessary and where things can be cut back to enable you to create a break even cashflow or better yet a positive cashflow.

We made changes like taking our daughter out of day care two days a week so I can spend more time with her and save some money in the process. By re-structuring the way we pay some of our expenses, we were able to generate more cashflow.

Positive Cashflow

If at the end of each month we have $500 left in our bank, then we have a positive cashflow of $500.

For a visual see the equation on the next page.

Positive Cashflow

	Monthly Cashflow
▪ Total Income	$4,000
▪ Total Expenses	$3,500
▪ Cashflow	$500

Graph 2.2

Positive cash flow for the month which would automatically pay off your Line of Credit (explained in more detail further in the book)

Example Total Income $4000pcm – All expenses pcm $3500 = cashflow $500

Doesn't sound like much, but you will soon see how this little amount will compound into massive savings by putting your hard-earned monies back in your pocket and not into those at the big financial institutions. It's our money, so let's keep it in our pocket and make it work for us and not simply hand it over to the banks because we think we have too. You would not simply give thousands of dollars away to a complete stranger each month so why are we happy to do this to the large financial institutions?

Again, coming back to changing our attitude towards our money, do not look at the one transaction as $500, look at the compounding effect and over the course of 4 months it is $2000. This can save $4000 every 4 months in interest payments (now that sounds better right?) therefore each year we will be saving around $12,000. This $12,000 in better in our pocket so we decided to get smart and put our money to work for us.

Break-even

If you are only able to get to a break-even scenario, this is good, and be sure to give yourself the credit you deserve for making the first step as this is always the hardest. Anything is better than a negative cashflow, so for now continue reading, educating yourself, starting to change your perception of money and your attitude to utilizing it to your advantage. Do not be scared to make changes in the way you use your money. Just remember you traded your time to earn it and you should not give it away so easily.

WE DID NOT START this banking strategy until we were in a positive cashflow position.

Rich people do not get rich by going to work for someone else day in day out. They make their money work for them and leverage the banks money to their advantage, which is exactly what my wife and I have done by utilizing this strategy. I am by far not a rich person, however that does not mean I cannot adapt and change my way of thinking.

If you are going to implement change then I would strongly suggest being patient, assess your cashflow situation, track and change spending habits if required and when you are confident in a positive cashflow, then implement the strategy and watch the savings build up. Start small and remember the compounding effect that all the small amounts total in that year.

Summary

→ Change attitude and perceptions towards our money

→ Negative cashflow No Velocity

→ Education and understanding seek advice do your own homework and understand the importance of your cashflow

→ Don't settle for giving away our hard-earned cash

→ Start small and build up (compound)

Chapter 3

Taking Control

Tracking money and spending (budget)

Before we began the terminal velocity strategy, we needed to be confident of where our money was going. Far too often we would say things like, 'I don't know where our money goes.' We had good jobs and yet still couldn't afford to go out for dinner or have a beer. We would look at other friends and wonder how they could always afford going out and enjoy themselves on a minimum wage or a single wage? Yes, they may not have the amount of debt which we acquired, but we still should have been able to afford a beer every now and then and not feel guilty about it!

Because of this, my wife and I knew we had to make changes to the way we used our money and refine what we were doing to track our spending.

In the beginning, we would try and track our monies by using an excel spreadsheet, input our expenses, tracking every little purchase through the month, but this just never seemed to help us. It became too time consuming and inconvenient. Looking back now, we were trying to fix something which we did not fully grasp or understand properly where we were going wrong. Firstly, our attitude had not changed. We simply thought that because we had well-paid jobs, we should automatically have cash left over each month, and if we didn't, then we were spending too much on things we didn't need. This was giving us the feelings of regret and guilt when we would go to the shops and buy things for ourselves because we were always feeling like we should not be spending. We did not know where or how to make changes to increase our monthly cashflow. We did not realize that by re-structuring the way some bills can be paid i.e. annually opposed to monthly, this would benefit our cashflow for the other 11 months of the year. Finally, our process of tracking our spending was all wrong.

We would track back through our bank statements each week to input each and every expense into the spreadsheet, trying to break every single expense down into the correct category and by doing this we actually made our finances seem too overwhelming and eventually gave up. It put us off making the effort to keep on top of it and as we had no real direction. It all seemed in vain as we were really unsure of what the end goal was and how to maximize any spare cash. Without knowing what the end goal was, we were unable to make the necessary changes to our finances.

Many times over the years, our New Year's Resolution was to sort out our finances and take control!

Did We Take Control?

In January 2019, after reading *The Bare Foot Investor*, this really opened our eyes to the fact something had to change, and we realized that simple is better. Again, an attitude adjustment. Basically, the strategy was a long-term investment and to open up different bank accounts (buckets) and then each week / month separate our income based on percentages. To do this, we needed to figure out what percentage we spent on bills, holidays, emergencies and saving (i.e. 60% of your wage allocated to bills, 20% allocated to emergencies, 10% to a holiday fund 10% to everyday spending / groceries etc) and all these buckets required a different bank account. We began to implement this strategy, had our bank accounts set up and began separating our monthly income. Through reading that book and implementing the strategy, it began to change our attitude to the way we looked at our money and where we were spending it. It was a great starting point to get into some good habits for tracking and setting aside our money on a regular basis.

Unfortunately, after my terminal prognosis in June 2019, instantly we realised this long-term strategy would no longer benefit us. What had this strategy of setting aside money each month really achieved?

By setting aside our money each week we were still trading our time for money which in my case now is potentially limited. I am still currently able to work however if the cancer continues to grow and spread, the day will come when I will not be able to work. You never expect news like this, especially at the age of 36.

However, it taught us the simpler and more convenient we could make something, the more likely we are to stick with it. It became clear what needed to change and how we could go about it, not to mention it gave us direction of where we were heading with an end goal, something which we could and would instantly see as a direct result of these changes. It showed us how a simple change in our finance structure could save us thousands.

From here, we looked back at what we were doing over the last 5 years in terms of tracking our money and what could be improved or adjusted and what could we do to simplify that process to really achieve what we set out to achieve all those years ago.

We asked ourselves, 'how can we make tracking our finances easier?' We have our monthly budget for everyday spending (Groceries, Dining etc) and the first simple step was to open a separate bank account where we would put aside our monthly everyday spending and this would enable us to track our spending without going into the minor details that made it time consuming and overwhelming. Simple right? Get a bank account and leave what is to be spent for the month or week only, then see if we spend more or less than our budget! Easy as that.

Attitude Adjustment

Once we started to change our attitude towards our money and our spending, we needed to take responsibility for our actions and what we were spending our money on and not to accept giving money to someone just because they said so. It was this change in attitude that made us start to look at our finances in a different light. I spoke with our home insurance company to get a better rate, instead of just accepting the first quote, shopped around for better electrical deals, but one thing jumped out at us and that was just how much we are paying to the bank in the way of interest every month.

I did more research into this and by implementing a new way of thinking and the new strategy, then it became clear to me that there was actually something we could do to maximize our saving and minimize the amount of monies we were simply giving away.

The main aspect to the strategy is to calculate the monthly cashflow and then utilizing this cashflow to our advantage, leveraging our monies against the large financial institutions and saving thousands of dollars in interest payments.

Focusing on our monthly cashflow we were able to make slight adjustments to generate more cashflow to benefit us.

Change is a scary thing

Making change is always a scary thing, and for many of us, this is the biggest challenge, especially when it comes to our finances. We are afraid we are going to lose our hard earned cash,, or it's not worth doing, or it must be a scam as there is no way to beat these large financial institutions, all coming back to our emotional feelings which relate to our money.

On the other hand, if we are too afraid to make changes and don't try anything different, then we will never get out of the vicious cycle which we are all trapped in by these large financial institutions.

In the beginning, our mortgage repayment to the bank was $2,863.00 per month and the interest was $1,953.66 therefore we were only paying $909.34 per month off the principal amount of the loan.

Once we realized how to utilize our cashflow, we simply needed to implement the following 3 steps.

Steps to Change

1. Creating the Spreadsheet (Simplifying) to track / identify our expenses

2. Opening the new everyday bank account

3. Opening / utilizing the banking tools correctly (line of Credit)

Step 1. Creating a Simplified Spreadsheet

We needed to create a spreadsheet showing all our unavoidable expenses:

→ Mortgage Repayments

→ Council Rates

→ Electricity

→ Water and Sewer

→ Car Registration

→ Car Insurance

→ Home Insurance

→ Monthly/Weekly everyday spending (Groceries, Dining etc)

Secondary Expenses

→ TV entertainment such as Netflix, Stan or similar

→ Phone & Internet

→ Day Care (if you have children)

→ Mobil Phone

→ Private Health / Life insurances

Household Income

→ Column with your weekly or monthly wage

→ Total Expenditures (to calculate the cashflow)

Step 2. Our bank accounts

Initially, my wife and I had around seven different bank accounts which we would then separate a percentage of our wage into each month trying to save our pennies. We now have only two.

1 — Existing main account.

This is the account which we have always had and where all the existing bills were paid, wages went into and then we would use this account for our everyday spending on things such as groceries, fuel for the car, dining out etc. By having all the bills and expenses coming and going from this account it was very difficult to track exactly where the money was going as we would need to check through the bank statements to confirm all this.

2 — Daily spending account.

This is the new account which we opened to separate our everyday spending money for the everyday things such as groceries, dining out, fuel, anything which we need for the week / month. This enables us to easily see how much we are spending on a monthly basis without going through the bank statements.

Here in Australia, there is a product called the Offset account which are bank accounts linked to home loans. Any monies in these accounts are offset against the outstanding loan amount and we are not charged interest on this figure. The problem with these accounts which we found is that the amount of interest actually saved is very minimal. For instance, in our circumstance we never had much money saved up and once I was diagnosed with cancer my family and friends were able to raise monies to help my family through this difficult time to the amount of around $50,000.Over the course of 6 months, with this amount of money sitting in the offset account, we saved around $4,763.80. Problem here is that the majority of us will not have a SPARE $50,000.00 sitting around in a bank account to offset our interest payments and the banks know this.

However, if you have the ability to open up one of these accounts at no extra cost then we might as well use this in conjunction with the strategy as the more we can save the better right? It's your hard-earned money and is better in your back pocket, not the banks.

Step 3. Line of credit (LOC)

This can be either a credit card or a Home Equity Line of Credit which is a product the bank has available, but we are blissfully unaware of, or at least I was. A line of credit is available to all of us and, if used correctly, we are able to leverage our monies against the bank and to save ourselves thousands in the process. My wife and I have always had credit cards, however we were using these tools incorrectly and in effect, these were hindering us and keeping us stuck in the cycle of spending and surviving month to month with our cashflow.

I found the banks were pushing us to either take out another loan or to get more offset accounts, as this is where they are making millions of dollars off everyday people like us who do the right thing and pay our mortgage monthly on a regular basis.

A little (and very important note): LOC is a line of credit which is secured against your property. Essentially, it is applying for another loan, in my case with a minimum amount of $20,000. So be aware that you must have at least enough equity in your house to successfully apply for a Home Equity LOC. You can say anything, like: 'I want a new bathroom, new car, extension on the house, consolidate other debits etc.' These words sound like music to the bank's ears. At the end of the day, they want you to have as much debt as possible so they can get as much interest as possible from you. You will need to be specific and persistent with these financial institutions as they will try their very best to convince you this LOC is bad and simply go for their other products such as the Offset or term loans. This was the case for me and other close friends who inquired about the LOC. If you do not have enough equity in your property, then simply using a credit card will still be beneficial

Once we had these two bank accounts set up and the new line of credit, we were now able to separate and re-arrange how we used our money and get it to start working for us.

Summary

→   Set budget

→   Set up excel spreadsheet to track expenses and calculate cashflow

→   Set up bank accounts (only 2)

→   Confirm which LOC is best suited to your individual situation

Chapter 4

Change can be a wonderful thing

Cashflow — Bills and expenses

Once we changed our mindset and attitude towards our money, we were able to see the importance of cashflow and how we could create more cashflow simply by restructuring some of our bills and the way we pay them, as well as implementing changes to the tools we had available.

The main turning point for me was realizing and understanding just how the cashflow could be leveraged against the financial institutions and to our great advantage! It was like the penny dropping and the realization that this type of strategy would work and was not just another one of these get rich quick schemes.

Now that we had created the everyday spending account and were separating our spending money, we were able to see our total expenses and confidently calculate our cashflow for the month, which would start working for us.

Change can be a wonderful thing.

To be honest, there was slight apprehension whether or not this was going to work. This was something that my wife and I started to look at once we really grasped the concept of the cashflow. It sounded simple at first, but then the fun began. We had to make some simple yet effective changes to create that little bit more cashflow, simply by restructuring the way we paid our bills. We had the same amount of bills; however, we created more cashflow per month.

All bills were set to be taken from the line of credit.

Mortgage

The only thing we changed to the mortgage repayment was the account it was coming out of and the time of the month in which this was paid. Because we are paid monthly, I changed this bill to be taken out on the 28th of each month (I will explain why further on) and to come out of the Line of Credit (LOC), not our personal account.

Council Rates

Usually paid quarterly. In the beginning, we would divide our quarterly bill of $407 by the three months and set aside $136 each month. Now we simply pay this quarterly and from the LOC.

Electricity

We pay our electricity bill monthly. If you pay on time, depending on the supplier, you get a small percentage deducted from the bill. On average, we have a household electricity bill of $200 per month. This is something we cannot get out of, but what we can do in an attempt to reduce the monthly bill is to be mindful of consumption within our home and shop around and try get a better deal either from our existing supplier or change to another. We aim to shop around on an annual basis. This bill is also now paid from the LOC.

Water and Sewerage

This is another bill which is usually paid quarterly. Initially, we would divide our quarterly bill of $160 by the three months and set aside $54 per month. Now we simply pay this quarterly and this is also paid from the LOC.

Car Registration

Our car registration for the year is approximately $800 and initially we would divide this by 12 months and then set aside $67 each month. Now we are paying this annually and this bill is also paid from the LOC.

Car Insurance

Our car insurance is around $690 per year and initially we would divide this by 12 months and set aside $58 per month. Now we are paying this annually and this bill is paid from the LOC.

Home Insurance

Our home insurance is around $2000 per year and initially we would divide this by 12 months and set aside $167 per month. Now this is paid annually and is paid from the LOC.

Monthly everyday spending (Groceries, Dining etc)

As this would vary, it was hard to try and set aside and track a weekly or monthly target as we had not yet simplified our spreadsheet or our way of tracking what we spent. Initially, all these expenses would be coming out of the same account, so trying to keep a track of this was a nightmare. Now we have the separate everyday spending account, it makes it very clear what we spend on our daily needs. This also helps keep on top of the expenses and spending on a daily basis. This cost can now be separated from our monthly bills as we automatically set aside a figure and transfer this to our everyday spending account.

If you have not noticed a small trend starting to appear, it is simply that what bills we can pay annually, we do so, and the quarterly bills are paid quarterly, all are coming from the LOC. This will mean that for the other 11 months of the year our cashflow will be increased. One important thing to note is that it may not be achievable to pay all your bills off at one time. It will all depend on your cashflow and ability to pay the LOC off, therefore you may need to select one bill at a time. When the cashflow slowly increases, more bills can be paid annually.

Secondary Expenses

These secondary expenses are what my wife and I have labelled as the expenses which we choose to have in our lives to make it more comfortable but they are the bills which we could potentially cut back on or go without, depending on our circumstances or way of life. There may be expenses which I have not listed below as these types will vary from person to person and be individual choices.

TV entertainment such as Netflix, Stan or similar

Usually a monthly bill but one that is fixed so we know what we are spending and is easy to keep track of. I currently spend $25 per month. This bill is paid from the LOC.

Phone & Internet

These can be a set monthly bill, depending on your contract with the provider and therefore you will need to see what the average spend is for your household and aim to keep within this budget. Our spend for the month is $95. Paid from the LOC.

Day Care (if you have children)

This can be an expensive but unavoidable cost if both adults in the home are working. My wife and I are that couple and my daughter has been going to day care since she was 10 months old.

Here in Australia, we were paying $1145 per month therefore we would divide by 4 (or 5 some months) and set aside $287 per week.

Because my wife was still working with her team in the UK, she suggested working from home twice a week to catch up with the time difference. This enabled us to reduce the days of our daughter being in care from 5 to 4. My wife looks after her in the morning and I look after her in the afternoon and night.

Since my diagnosis, we have taken our daughter out of school for 2 days a week so I can spend that little bit more time with her and boost our cashflow that little bit more. This has helped obviously and now our monthly bill has been reduced to $750 therefore initially we would set aside weekly bill of $188 per week. Now we pay this monthly bill and from the LOC

Mobile Phone

Just about everyone on the planet now has one of these. Our contract is $88 per month, which is paid monthly and from the LOC.

Private Health

My wife and I have private health insurance which now in my case, I am glad we did. Once I received my cancer diagnosis, I went through chemotherapy, major operations, doctors' appointments, scans etc. The list goes on and so do the cost for these items. For example, the surgeon which carried out my major operation estimated the cost for the surgery to be over $100,000. If I did not have private health insurance, I would be on the waiting list to go through the public system.

Our premium for the Private health insurance was $396 per month and this covered myself, my wife and daughter. The yearly cost is $4,752. We would put aside the $396 per month. This being a fixed bill should not change and therefore easy to track. Now this bill is paid annually and paid from the LOC.

Life insurances

Our life insurance is now split, some coming from our super fund and the rest from our wage each month. Our monthly expense was $220 per month with a yearly bill of $1320 each. This is a fixed bill so again is one that is easily tracked. I spoke with the insurance company and if we were to pay this annually, then we would get a further 8% discount so needless to say this bill is now paid annually and paid from the LOC.

There may be times throughout the year where we spend a little more on the monthly bills, but also there will be times where we do not spend the allocated amount, so we should not be too hard on ourselves.

You do need to keep track and if you notice an increase in the spending on a regular basis, then the budget will need to be adjusted to suit and you may need to cut back in other areas.

Expenses

If we were to set aside money each month for our bills, we would have to do the following:

Council – $136

Electricity — $200

Water & Sewer — $54

Day Care — $750

Tv Entertainment — $25

Phone & Internet – $95

Car Registration — $67 (monthly)

Car Insurance — $58 (monthly)

Home Insurance — $167 (monthly)

Life Insurance — $220 (monthly)

Private Health Insurance — $396 (monthly)

Total — $2,168.00 per month.

We cannot avoid these costs. What could we do with these bills to create some cashflow and get our money working in our favour?

The answer was right in front of us, but it was hard to see without the right mindset and understanding what needs to change to get our money working for us instead of us working for the money.

We were able to pay the majority of the bills annually, however each individual circumstance will be different therefore it's important to consider your own cashflow and what you can afford to pay off and how quickly. It wasn't viable for us to pay all of the expenses yearly at first, but over time we will get there. The more bulk payments onto the mortgage save us money and create that little bit more cashflow.

Expenses Paying Annually and *creating cashflow*

After paying the bills we could annually, for 11 months of the year we are leveraging our money to pay back the LOC and creating cashflow to work for us. We are left with the following bills which will need to be paid on a monthly or quarterly basis

Council – $136 (month)

Electricity — $200 (month)

Water & Sewer — $54 (month)

Day Care — $750 (month)

Tv Entertainment — $25 (month)

Phone & Internet – $95 (month)

Total — $ 1,260.00

Generating Cashflow of $908 per month

Again, it may not be a viable option to pay all the bills from the line of credit in the beginning as all you will be doing is paying down your bills. I have found a good target for paying down the line of credit should be achievable within 3-6 months, as this will enable us to get the most benefit from this strategy. If we are able to pay back $2,000 over 3 months, then we can do this 4 times per year with a total of $8,000 additional paid off the principal and saving us around $16,000 in interest payments to the bank. Or $2,000 over 4 months then this can be done 3 times per year for a total of $6,000 additional off the principal and around $12,000 saved in interest payments. We are aiming to get as many bulk payments onto our mortgage, paying off the principal each time, and by doing this we are avoiding paying excess interest repayments.

Each time there has been a bulk payment onto our mortgage, my wife and I have reduced the monthly mortgage repayment. We put a $16,000 bulk payment onto the mortgage which saved us $75 dollars per month (over the year this is $900 in our pocket), but the big saving is the fact we just saved ourselves around $30,000 in interest payments to the bank! This will slowly enable us to pay back the line of credit that little bit faster each time we make the bulk payments and eventually we created more and more cashflow each month.

Depending on your financial situation, dropping your repayment is something that does not have to be done. You should look at the repayments and then make a judgment on what you would prefer and more importantly what works better with your situation, as everyone will have different circumstances. Options are to either reduce the loan repayments or keep them the same. Due to our circumstance and my cancer diagnosis, we chose to reduce the repayments to increase cash flow.

If you were to keep the re-payments the same, you will notice each bulk payment onto the mortgage will cut down the life of the loan. Instead of a 30-year loan you can cut years of the loan overnight depending on your cashflow and the size of your bulk payment.

Paying Expenses

Once we determined which bills would be paid off monthly/ quarterly or annually, we then set up all the expenses to be paid from the LOC account. So, if your cashflow was $500 per month then without doing anything the LOC will be paid off by $500 each month (total income into the LOC – All expenses out of the LOC).

Banking Strategy - 2019	
Expense	
Vary Home Loan	weekly
Fix Home Loan	monthly
Day Care	monthly
Swim Lessons Giulia	quarterly
Billys Buddies	monthly
Yoga	quarterly
Tolls	monthly
Pet Insurance	monthly
Mobile Cristine	monthly
Netflix & Stan	monthly
Apple Apps	monthly
Car Insurance	yearly (5th Jui)
Car Rego	yearly 27th Nov
Roadside Assistance	yearly (29th Nov)
Home Insurance	yearly (16th Aug 19)
CBHS Private Health	yearly (28th Aug 20)
Clearview Life Insurances (Cristine)	yearly (30th May 20)
Clearview Life Insurances (Michael)	yearly (30th May 20)
Wealth Package	yearly (25th Jan 20)
Michaels Spending	monthly
Cristine Spending	monthly
VLOC Interest	monthly
Total	

Graph 4.1 – Changing bills to get our money working better for us

The above examples of expenses are ones which my wife

and I have. Individuals will have other expenses which I may not have mentioned here in the book, however the same principals can apply. Asses your bills and expenses and see where you can pay yearly to create more cashflow for the other 11 months of the year.

More cashflow in your pocket helps pay the Line of Credit (LOC) quicker and therefore will enable you to pay more bulk payments directly off the principal of the loan and saving thousands.

Re-structuring Steps

1. We set up our total income to all be paid into the LOC account (either the Credit Card account or the LOC).

2. Once all our income was sent to the LOC then we created one transfer each month to our everyday spending account with our agreed budget amount.

3. All expenses were taken from the LOC account (later in the month the better as this will again cut down on the interest charged on the LOC).

If you are using the credit card as your LOC, then by setting up the payments like this you will also be getting rid of the need to pay a monthly Credit Card bill as all your wage is being paid onto the Credit Card, therefore you have generated a little more cashflow straight away. Another change my wife and I made was to get as many bills paid at the end of the month. This will mean for the majority of the month we will be paying interest on the smallest amount possible from the LOC and right at the end of the month, all the bills will be taken from the LOC and we will then pay interest on the larger amount only for a short period. I have changed all bills to be taken from the 28th of each month (we chose the 28th only because this is the last day in February and every 4 years Feb has 29 days) as this saves us money on the interest we will be paying from the line of credit. We still must pay interest on the monies owed from the line of credit, but this interest is calculated differently to our home or fixed loans and therefore the amount of interest is minimal.

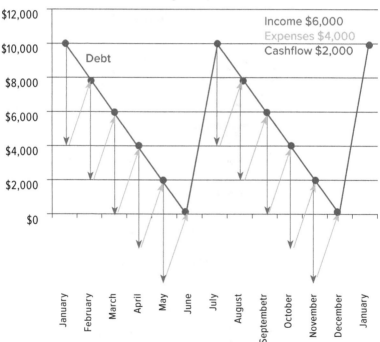

Monthly Overview

Graph 4.2
Principle of paying down the LOC
and cashflow working for us

Limit type	Limit	Start		Balance	Debit interest rate
Overdraft	$20,000.00	01/05/2019		$0 to $20,000	4.73% p.a.
		For balances over this approved limit, the debit excess interest rate of 17.94% p.a. applies			

Taxes & interest	This accrual period ⓘ	2018-19 financial year	2019-20 financial year
Loan interest	$62.23 DR	$7.08 DR	$186.33 DR

Graph 4.3

This is a snip from my personal banking web site taken November 2019. We have only paid $186.33 in interest and we have managed to pay off $36,000 off the principal! This would equate to a saving of around $70,000 in interest payments to the bank

‹ Bills and upcoming payments +
Next 7 days
Michael Spending $950.00   2 days - Scheduled
Future
Michael Spending $950.00   16 Feb - Scheduled
Michael Spending $950.00   16 Mar - Scheduled
Michael Spending $950.00   16 Apr - Scheduled
Michael Spending $950.00   16 May - Scheduled
Michael Spending $950.00   16 Jun - Scheduled

Graph 4.4

Monthly direct debit from LOC to the daily spending account, once this is set up, we don't have to do anything else just leave it and forget about it.

My wife and I made the first bulk payment of $20,000 to our mortgage three weeks after my Esophagectomy surgery and we have only paid this minimal amount of interest and saved straight away around $38,000 of interest payments! This is money saved and in our pocket.

Tracking Our Progress

We needed to stay on track with our budget, and to do this we simply crossed off and checked our expenditures throughout the month as they came in.

This should not be something which takes a lot of time, it is simply ensuring that when the bills come in and go out, they are as per the predicted costs which would be in the budget spreadsheet.

The easiest way I have found to do this is simply by leaving all the information in the spreadsheet in red coloured text and when I confirm these costs, I change the text to black.

We can then see if we are on target with our cashflow prediction. It becomes a strategy that once in motion will automatically happen and we will not have to do anything until the time when our LOC balance has been paid all the way down to a zero balance. When I say automatically, I mean we all get paid for our day jobs and pay bills on a regular basis, therefore by simply re-structuring and managing the way we pay our bills the LOC will automatically be getting paid back to zero whilst we go about our daily tasks nothing has changed.

Once the LOC has been paid back to zero balance, we simply make the next bulk payment to the loan account and again see the instant result and savings we have just made all whilst using the banks money.

The results were immediate; we were able to calculate what we have saved ourselves in terms of the interest payments and this was great motivation. I have never been able to save $20,000, not even $10,000, and if I had saved up this amount of money before changing my attitude, I'm sure putting it all onto the mortgage would not have been the first option. More likely I would have tended to treat myself to a holiday or something rewarding. However, once I had opened a LOC Account, I was able to put $20,000 of the BANKS money directly onto my mortgage, saving myself a whopping $38,000 in interest payments over the life of the loan. I am still in the same amount of debt however *it has been transferred from amortized interest onto the simple interest loan.*

Expense	May	Jun	Jul	Aug	Sep	Oct	Nov	Dec
Council Rates	$ -	$ -	$ -	$ 407.15	$ -	$ -	$ 420.00	$ -
Electricity (Origin)	$ 179.03	$ 167.92	$ 270.24	$ 220.30	$ 180.00	$ 180.00	$ 180.00	$ 180.00
Water & Sewage (Urban Utilities)	$ 149.87	$ -	$ 177.66	$ -	$ 150.00	$ -	$ -	$ -
SEQ Waste Mgt	$ -	$ -	$ -	$ 70.00	$ -	$ -	$ -	$ 70.00
Pool	$ -	$ -	$ -	$ -	$ -	$ -	$ -	$ -
Phone + Internet (Telstra)	$ 93.30	$ 105.87	$ 79.33	$ 95.00	$ 95.00	$ 95.00	$ 95.00	$ 95.00
Vary Home Loan	$ 825.00	$ 640.00	$ 640.00	$ 745.00	$ 596.00	$ 596.00	$ 745.00	$ 596.00
Vary Home Loan (was originally fixed)	$ 2,863.00	$ 2,863.00	$ 1,500.00	$ 1,449.00	$ 1,449.00	$ 1,449.00	$ 1,449.00	$ 1,449.00
Day Care	$ 1,145.00	$ 600.00	$ 1,179.02	$ 750.00	$ 750.00	$ 750.00	$ 750.00	$ 750.00
Swim Lessons	$ 102.00	$ -	$ 48.00	$ -	$ -	$ -	$ -	$ -
Billys Buddies	$ 48.00	$ 48.00	$ 250.00	$ 61.30	$ 50.00	$ 50.00	$ 61.30	$ 50.00
Yoga	$ -	$ -	$ -	$ -	$ -	$ 150.00	$ -	$ 150.00
Tolls	$ 180.00	$ -	$ -	$ 100.00	$ -	$ -	$ 100.00	$ -
Pet Insurance	$ 32.39	$ 32.39	$ 32.39	$ 32.39	$ 32.39	$ 32.39	$ 32.39	$ 32.39
Mobile Cristine	$ 117.58	$ 95.25	$ 88.99	$ 88.99	$ 95.00	$ 95.00	$ 95.00	$ 95.00
	$ 25.00	$ 25.00	$ 25.00	$ -	$ -	$ -	$ -	$ -
Car Insurance	$ 58.00	$ 58.00	$ 58.00	$ -	$ -	$ -	$ -	$ -
Car Rego	$ 67.00	$ 67.00	$ 67.00	$ -	$ -	$ -	$ -	$ -
Home Insurance	$ 167.00	$ 167.00	$ 167.00	$ -	$ -	$ -	$ -	$ -
Private Health/ Gold Hosp (no extras)	$ 396.03	$ 396.03	$ 396.03	$ 169.73	$ -	$ -	$ -	$ -
Life Insurances (Cristine)	$ 220.00	$ 220.00	$ 220.00	$ -	$ -	$ -	$ -	$ -
Life Insurances (Michael)	$ 220.00	$ 220.00	$ 220.00	$ -	$ -	$ -	$ -	$ -
Wealth Package	$ -	$ -	$ -	$ -	$ -	$ -	$ -	$ -
Michaels Spending	$ 950.00	$ 950.00	$ 950.00	$ 950.00	$ 950.00	$ 950.00	$ 950.00	$ 950.00
Cristine Spending	$ 950.00	$ 950.00	$ 950.00	$ 950.00	$ 950.00	$ 950.00	$ 950.00	$ 950.00
VLOC Interest	$ -	$ -	$ 40.92	$ 36.88	$ 31.43	$ -	$ -	$ -
Total	$ 8,788.20	$ 7,605.46	$ 7,584.58	$ 6,125.74	$ 5,328.82	$ 5,297.39	$ 5,827.69	$ 5,367.39

Graph 4.5 – Showing expenses and tracking – Notice once bills were paid annually the expenses decrease which increases the cashflow for the month

Summary

→   Total income to be put into the LOC (helps minimize the interest we pay on the LOC)

→   Set regular transaction from LOC to everyday spending account

→   Asses your monthly bills

→   Asses yearly bills

→   Assess cashflow and calculate what you can afford to pay back in a timely manner (over 3-6 months)

→   Change bills to yearly or quarterly and avoid setting aside money weekly / monthly into a separate account

→   Set all bills to come from the LOC at the end of the month including the larger yearly bills.

Chapter 5

Insurance

Making sure we're covered

Getting the right advice on insurance is crucial, as it can be a very scary and muddy field to navigate. In my case, I never had the right insurances in place, and it was too late to change my cover after the diagnosis. Now I am stuck with what little insurance I had and have to deal with the consequences and what effect this has on my family. This is my biggest regret to date. The stress and pressure this places on my wife is heartbreaking to see and there is nothing I can do to change this.

Ironically, we were due to sit down and discuss and address our insurances the night after the diagnosis back in January, however for me this was too late.

My wife and I sat down with a friend who is a specialist in the insurance business who helped us obtain the right cover. Courtney from ELBON FINANCIAL SERVICES who specialises in wealth creation, helped us a great deal and along the way we found out a lot of unsettling things which could happen if we did not have the right cover in place.

In my scenario, I found out the hard way the implications of not having the correct cover, as I had minimal life insurance through my super fund which was nowhere near sufficient for the amount of debt we were in.

As I was always young, fit and healthy, I never had the right attitude towards my insurances, partly because I was arrogant and never thought something like this would happen to me.

I was invincible.

Because of my arrogance, and insufficient insurance, this now adds to the financial pressure which I feel I could be leaving behind for my wife to deal with, which is a horrible feeling.

When it comes to personal insurance cover, it is important to know what you are paying for and ensuring you have a strategy in place.

After speaking with Courtney on many occasions, I would like to share some information which she was kind enough to write for this book.

Insurance

When it comes to personal insurance cover it is important to know what you are paying for.

All of the information provided here is of a general nature and doesn't take in to account your own personal circumstances or situation. You should seek advice to make sure you have the right plan in place that suits your circumstances.

If you think insurances is simple, I urge you to reconsider your thinking. The advantage of engaging with an adviser is not only to get a handle on things at the beginning of obtaining insurance cover but also the advantage of having a positive outcome at claim time.

The response I have heard too many times, I have my insurance cover provided under my work super it will be alright! Have you ever even thought to look at what this is costing and what it provides at the time of a medical catastrophe?

Most people have not truly investigated their insurance needs until after they get a mortgage, have kids, or reach 40+. If you take away one important piece of advice here, it pays to get good advice at any age but preferably when you have good health, this usually means before you have the picket fence, the kids and the dog!

When you apply for insurance, insurers can exclude pre-existing conditions, add a loading to the premium you pay, exclude benefits or decline to offer you cover based on your occupation, medical history, even your family history. It does not seem important until you need it. Putting personal insurances in place will be the best decision you make to protect yourself, protect your income, your family and your family's financial future.

I am not saying having cover under super is bad, it is better than nothing, but it is a misconception that it is always cheaper, and it does not necessarily mean it is better. You get what you pay for. Although many don't even consider that as the cost is not coming from their pocket. Your superannuation fund is paying it in many circumstances, eroding away at your retirement savings!

Group insurance provided via your super fund is a basic product usually with minimal ancillary benefits, the terms of the contract can be changed at any time, the policy is cancellable and pre-existing conditions can be excluded without you even realising. These are just a few issues to note and without doing a full analysis of what your provider offers on a regular basis you will be none the wiser.

The Different Types of Insurance

Life/Term/Death Insurance

Life insurance can pay on death or terminal illness. If a terminal illness is diagnosed giving you less than 12 months to live, you need to have two doctors to sign off that you will not survive past 12 months which may qualify you for early access to this benefit. It can give the recipient a sense of peace of mind being able to take control of how to position themselves and family. This may assist with medical bills, pay off debt, investing the funds for future income for the family or to achieve a few things they wish to tick off the bucket list. Life insurance is available inside and outside of superannuation however if held inside superannuation taxes may apply if paid to non-dependants.

Total and Permanent Disability (TPD) Insurance

TPD has two different contracts available Own occupation and Any Occupation.

Own occupation covers you as long as you are unable to work in your own occupation or profession (i.e. the job you have currently been working in).

Any occupation covers you if you unable to return to the workforce in any occupation that is suited to your education, training or experience. This is a much broader definition that's harder to prove.

The best option though more costly is the own occupation definition. It does give a greater chance at claim time without having the restraints of the Any Occupation guidelines. Any Occupation can mean that you can return to work in any job that you are suited to by education, training or experience.

Start to think of all of the jobs you have had over the years and that is what an insurer will be making an assessment on at claim time. This is the contract available under super or provided as a default under group insurance.

Own Occupation is not available under super but there are funding strategies to assist financial restraints by paying for your cover using superannuation funds.

Trauma/ Recovery/ Critical Illness Insurance

Trauma cover pays a lump sum benefit to the policy holder on the diagnosis of cancer, heart attack, stroke, bypass operation and over 40 other conditions. You do have to meet the definition of a claimable event and survive a specified period of time past the diagnosis of an event.

Also, there is a waiting period of 90 days for some trauma events to avoid people taking out insurance after a diagnosis of a claimable event.

Having been in this business for almost 20 years, hands down this would be the most claimed benefit in my experience alongside income protection. It always surprises me when people tell me that they have never heard of Trauma insurance. I always recommend this cover and see it as a non-negotiable when putting a plan together for clients.

I am sure it is no surprise that cancer is the most claimed event. According to Zurich's 2018 Cost of Care study, one in every three Australian men and one in every four Australian women will be diagnosed with cancer by the age of 75 years.

What sets Trauma cover apart from Total and Permanent Disability cover (TPD) is that there is no requirement to be totally and permanently disabled and never likely to go back to work.

Often after cancer or a heart attack for example, a patient can recover but not be permanently incapacitated. They need financial assistance to top up their loss of income, pay their medical expenses or to have the option to have private rather than public treatment.

In the last 12 months I have had two clients faced with a trauma event whilst formulating advice and one diagnosed whilst serving the waiting period. I cannot stress enough, the benefit of having Trauma insurance. Even if you cannot afford what you should have, minimum cover could assist with expenses.

Childs Trauma Cover

Childs Trauma cover will pay a lump sum if the policy holder's child is diagnosed with a specified trauma condition is diagnosed with a terminal illness or dies. This cover is to assist with the medical costs of a very sick child, home modifications to the family home or for the policy holder to stop work to be with their child. This is a low cost addition to a policy and the ownership can be transferred when the child becomes an adult.

Income Protection

What is your most important asset — your income? It provides you with the ability to live a certain lifestyle or not. Income Protection provides an income in the event the policy holder is unable to perform their duties of employment due to an accident or sickness. It usually provides you with 75% of your income. It will never provide 100% as no one would want to go back to work.

Income Protection is currently a mine field and there have been so many options available; basic no frills, Standard with some additions and Plus contracts with a comprehensive list of additional benefits but contracts are set to change as of March 2020 in the attempt to make income protection insurance sustainable for the policy holders.

The Australian Prudential Regulation Authority (APRA) has launched intervention into the life insurance market in response to ongoing heavy losses in respect of individual disability income insurance. I guess when the Life insurance companies have collectively lost just under $5 billion dollars over the last 5 years something needed to be done to make the industry more sustainable.

The generous benefit of having an income protection policy to pay you a monthly benefit up to age 65/70 years may no longer be an option depending on how APRA implements these changes. One thing we do know is that Agreed Value contacts offering locked in monthly benefits, Indemnity contracts looking to assess your pre-disability income based on your best annual income in the previous 3 years prior to your disability will be gone.

The increases to premiums in the future is unknown. If you can afford to maintain your current income protection contracts, this is most likely what I would consider.

New style income protection policies will only be available from March 2020 and will look to assess your pre-disability income based on your income 12 months prior to your disability, with benefit periods potentially being restricted to 2 or 5 years.

It is unknown how this will affect the cost to the customer at this time, but one thing is for certain, the Income Protection landscape is changing, and it may mean needing to reconsider how all these different types of insurance work together. So many things can hinge on this. Will you be able to return to work in some form? Part time, a less involved job, a change of career, if at all? How will it affect your lifestyle, pay the mortgage, buy groceries etc.

If you wish to explore more about the looming changes you can read the APRA media release from 2 December 2019.

https://www.apra.gov.au/news-and-publications/ apra-intervenes-to-improve-sustainability-of- individual-disability-income

I've got insurance, now what?

OK, you have insurance now, great! But what happens if you die? You need to nominate who is to get your insurance payment. This is usually done when taking out insurance cover and is legally binding. If you do not nominate a beneficiary, the proceeds of your policy will be paid to your estate and distributed according to your Will if you have one

This leads us into a whole other area, being estate planning of having an up to date Will, Power of Attorney and Health Directive plus Guardianship of children under the age of 18 years. A solicitor can assist you in this area.

I would suggest you seek advice to make sure you have the right plan in place that suits your circumstances.

What would you like to happen if you died tomorrow, were diagnosed with cancer, became ill or had an accident and couldn't work? What would happen to your family? You insure your car, house, boat etc, why not you?

Courtney, Elbon Financial Services

After sitting down with Courtney and going through all these options, sadly I discovered that mine and my wife's insurances were inadequate, and it was now too late to change anything for me. A few days after our initial meeting with Courtney, my wife discovered a lump in her breast which was a crushing blow at this point in our lives, but thankfully the biopsy came back all clear. This was probably the worst two weeks of my life, as I could not bear the thought of something happening to my wife and leaving our daughter orphaned. With this recent scare with my wife, it also meant that all insurers bar one would fully insure her. Courtney was able to re-arrange my wife's insurances to ensure if something happens to her, our four-year-old daughter would be covered for things such as schooling. We were one of those people who had never heard of Trauma insurance and needless to say, my wife and daughter are now covered.

Since my cancer diagnosis, there was only one insurance company who was willing to insure me for accidental death cover only, which I have since taken out. If we have the right insurances in place, we pay a fee each month and then in the event something should happen, we will be covered to a certain degree.

Insurance is, in my opinion, is a necessary evil. We don't need it until something life changing happens. We pay a premium for years and hopefully never need it, but in the event we do, then let me tell you having the correct insurances in place will take a massive burden off your shoulders and the loved ones around you, so please, if you are thinking of getting rid of your insurances due to the high premium, then reconsider. Reach out to Courtney or a trusted wealth protection specialist and see what type of cover might be best suited to your individual situation. You do not want to be in my shoes!

A few years back, my wife and I spoke about sorting out our Will, but at the time, making decisions such as would we be cremated, buried, who would look after our daughter etc were too uncomfortable, so we simply brushed it aside. We never prioritized this because the thought of death was not going to be for a long while yet, therefore this was not a necessity and never completed.

In my experience, people in general avoid discussing topics regarding death, as it makes us all very uncomfortable and yet this is the only certainty we have in life. I would urge anyone to have these uncomfortable discussions before they are in a situation like mine, as this just adds to the pressures and morbid feelings, knowing the end is potentially just around the corner. To now discuss my death and burial is like adding salt to the wound. I could not hide from this anymore and came to the realization that the more I can plan now, it will only assist my family, when the worst case is realized. In my opinion, it would be selfish of me to bury my head in the sand and ignore this, as I would be leaving another problem for my family to deal with.

Courtney was able to provide details of a solicitor which my wife and I went to see to complete our Will, Power of Attorney and Health Directive, plus Guardianship of minor (under 18) children.

Ask yourself this question; 'If you were injured or fall ill tomorrow and would not be able to exchange time for money (not be able to work) where would this leave you and your family? Would your wife or husband be covered for all the debt you are in? Would your child or children have access to better education or simply have the lifestyle you set out to provide?'

If not, then do something about it.

Now.

Summary

→ Prioritize your health and Insure your most valuable asset (Your Life)

→ Seek advice on your current situation of insurances

→ Consider what needs to be insured (Education, Mortgages, Debts, Lifestyle etc)

→ There are strategies which can be put in place to ensure your covered for the right amount and the correct policies

→ Discuss your Will and ensure you plan ahead no matter how uncomfortable this may make you feel

Courtney Noble

Authorised Representative of
Affinia Financial Advisers Limited
ABN 13 085 335 397 & AFSL 237857
ELBON FINANCIAL SERVICES
50 Raeside Street, Westlake 4074
PO Box 345, Mt Ommaney 4074
Phone: 07 3376 4100
Email: courtney@elbon.com.au

Beginning Of the Journey – myself family in the days following the initial diagnosis at home still coming to terms with the news.

Day my hair fell out – three weeks into my chemo I noticed a big chunk of hair fall out and it just happened to be the same time my friends Dylan, Frank and Justin (facing page) were visiting. I decided to take matters into my own hands and shave my head and be proud of this moment. All the guys decided to shave their heads in support which was great as Giulia got in on the action and we made light of this situation.

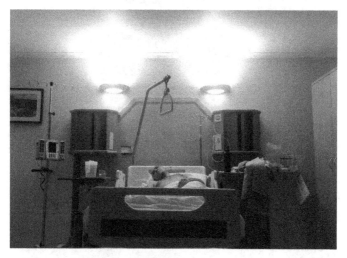

*Me in hospital recovering from a PICC Line infection – this
was just before the last chemo treatment and I spent a week
in hospital due to the infection, connected to antibiotics and
numerous other drugs. I managed to stay on target and had the
last chemo as per the schedule, the doctors wanted to delay
however I was adamant I wanted to finish.*

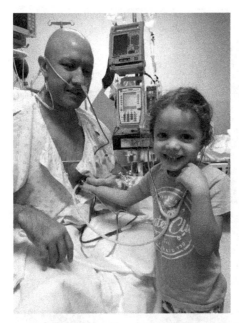

Intensive Care following my major surgery with my Little doctor in the making – Giulia was in the Intensive Care Unit as soon as I was awake from surgery. We encouraged her to be aware of what was happening and never lied to her about the situation.

Day of the prognosis – following the prognosis and being told I could have 6 months to live by the doctors we headed to the beach to spend the day as a family to create memories.

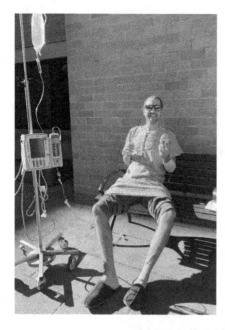

Recovering in hospital following the emergency Bowel Obstruction operation – this was me at my lowest point. The doctors did not pick up on the obstruction and I truly felt like this was the beginning of the end. The day after the surgery I was up and about the hospital enjoying an ice cream in the sun with my family.

Writing the book – whilst on holiday at Binna Burra Lodge I continued to work on this book and write in its beautiful and tranquil setting. Unfortunately two weeks later Binna Burra was destroyed due to the bushfires.

Chapter 6

Good Little Savers

Good v Bad Debt

Is there such thing as a good debt?

The key to reducing debt is understanding debt, accepting debt and then making debt work for you.

From an early age we are all taught about saving our pennies and handing our money over to the banks to keep it safe. It all started for me when I opened my savings account in primary school. From that point on, I was taught to go to work save my money and one day buy a home of my own.

Going through school, we are all taught the basics; Math, English, Science, History, but never anything about clearing debit or managing our finances. If you ask me, this would be a real-life skill which would benefit many of us. The catch is all the information we are given from this early age is what the banks and financial institutions want us to know.

We are told we must go to school to get a good education so we can then get a good well-paid job, and live out the great Australian dream; buy a car, find a partner settle down, buy a house, start a family and live happily ever after!

So, let me translate this.

Go to school and get the good education so you can then go to university and get a student loan, buy your first car (another loan), get married (pay for the wedding), have kids which inevitably cost money, then the big one; buy your first home by entering a large non tax deductible loan over 30 years and always be struggling to pay and potentially never pay off in full.

Most of us, myself included, were forever either refinancing or using the redraw facility to upgrade or extend our home or consolidate credit card loans. By doing this, we were adding more time onto the loan and the bank was gaining thousands in interest payments.

Each time we are refinancing and consolidating our loans, we are unknowingly (at least I did not know or realize) staying at the beginning of our loans, which is the part where we are paying the most interest to the banks. If we do finally pay off our initial mortgage, we will pay almost double, if not more than double our initial borrowed amount. This is because we pay back the interest first before we effectively pay off our portion of the loan and finally owning our home. These big banks are sitting back laughing at us little guys as we struggle along and simply pay our mortgage each month, whilst they are making a fortune on the side.

I am not saying that getting a good education is not important. In fact, it is important to go to school and get the best education possible. As I always tell my daughter, knowledge is power! Knowledge is something that no one can take away from us, so the more we educate ourselves, the better our chances are of succeeding in life. If we educate ourselves and use these financial tools available to us in the correct way, then these large debts that we will inevitably acquire throughout our lives does not have to be so daunting or need to rule our lives. We can potentially have these paid off in a fraction of the time, which will then free us up to do the things we really love. It can have the potential to cut down the stress levels and potentially have a better effect on our health in the long term.

My sister and I saved our money for many years to enable us to purchase our first property which set us back $327,000. My sister and I worked hard, paid our mortgage on time and were actually paying more than the required monthly repayment each week. We were also paying the loan weekly instead of monthly to save on interest payments, but still over the eight year period we had the loan, we only paid off around $69,000 off the principal, leaving us owing around $258,000 at the time of the sale. In 2017, we were able to sell this property for $662,000, which was a great result, enabling my sister and I to upgrade and get our own homes respectively.

I withdrew some of the equity prior to the sale of the house in Australia and used this money towards a deposit to buy a small Terraced house in the outskirts of London with my wife when things were looking up. Over the course of two years, we installed a new kitchen, bathroom and painted the inside of the property and other minor renovation works, which I was able to carry out myself, saving thousands on labor costs. It was a great feeling to be paying off our own property instead of paying rent and inevitably paying someone else's property off. At the time, we did not know of this strategy and we weren't educated in how to use our money or the lending tools available. Now looking back, it makes me angry as we could still have that property and be making money through rent ourselves. Instead, the reality is that when we relocated back to Australia, we had to sell the UK home, due to the fact we did not manage to pay much of the principal down and the rent would not cover the mortgage and we could no longer afford to send money back to the UK. On the sale, we did make a little money due to appreciation of the property and our renovation works overall (we made around £30,000 (pounds) profit, totaling around $100,000 AUD).

Excitedly thinking that this $100,000 would be a lot of money to pay onto our home mortgage here in Australia, I went into my bank and spoke with the mortgage advisor who informed me if I was to put this on my mortgage, I would save around $4,000 per year on my payments. I was stunned and didn't like the sound of paying $100,000 of my own money to save $4,000. I asked what else could I do with the money to best benefit my family and I was told that if I got an investment property here in Australia, the bank would give me a better rate on my existing home loan and I would still be saving $4,000 per year. I was then told I had to spend money to make money! My reply was that we were already at our maximum capacity in terms of debt, but if the bank was willing to give me more money, than we were going to take it! Sounds crazy and at the time it was a big risk for my wife and I, but in the hope we could pull it off and not lose everything in the process, we said yes to the investment loan and off we went to find an investment property.

From here, my wife and I invested money into property, got a better rate on our home loan and continued struggling to pay our bills. All too often we found ourselves in this predicament, struggling to pay bills and the only way to get a head is to work harder and trade more of our precious time for money.

Acquiring debt through our lives is something that we should not fear as there is such thing as good debt. For me, investing in property is something which I consider good debt as the property market has the potential to go up through appreciation (also still has the potential to come down with the market), and in the long term has great potential to make us money, either through capital gains or rental income from investment properties. Also, if we are able to pay off these properties, then these are ours and will also benefit us in retirement rather than only relying on our super, as this may not always be enough for our situation or lifestyle.

Buying a home is something which we should not fear as paying off something that in the long run could be ours and which no one can take away from us would be a great feeling, and I can only imagine the day when our home is fully paid off! It would be a huge burden removed from our shoulders.

Good Debt

*Google "**Good debt**" is typically defined as **debt** used to finance something that will increase in value in the future. Mortgage **debt** is a classic example: You get a mortgage to buy a house today, and in 30 years, when you've paid off that mortgage, the house could be worth two or three times its purchase price."*

In my opinion, good debt would be considered as being a loan for something which has the potential to make us money(buying your own home, business loan, student loan), investing in ourselves or for something which would be able to make you money.

Buying into property has the potential to make us money through the property appreciating in value, just like what happened with my sister and I and then also to my wife and I in the UK. Over the course of time property tends to go up, come down and then back up. This is what is called the property cycle. Therefore, investing in property is seen as a good debt and could make us money in the long run. However, be warned at the same time as it can go up in value it can also go down in value. Therefore, this is something which needs to be taken seriously.

It is critical to carry out your own due diligence, research and case study before committing as there are many different investment strategies which need to be considered before jumping into investing.

When you're looking for your first home, this is an exciting time and one we should not have to fear, but we do as the thought of buying into a loan for what might be the rest of our lives is scary.

If you're a tradesmen or tradeswomen then your good debt may be a vehicle for your business, or your tools. These are a necessary cost which have the potential to make you money, as without these items we would not be able to work and make money. These types of loans (e.g. car loans) are also usually calculated just like the home loans and therefore can be cleared using this strategy and free you of the debt faster whilst saving thousands in the process.

If you have just finished school and then plan to head off to Uni to get a degree, then you may have to get a student loan to cover cost of the course and will be locked in to paying this off when you start to work. These loans can be cleared by using this strategy and again, you will be amazed at the amount of interest you will save in the process, not to mention the amount of time which will be cut from the loan by using the tools available from the large financial institutions.

Bad Debt

I was pushing my health and loved ones aside and it has taken a terminal illness for me to realize just how stupid I was wasting money and time paying off bad debt. Looking back, I realize just how much time I missed with the love of my life and now being told I would have 6-12 months to live. Was all that time away really worth it, and for what, as I still have large debts to pay?

Bad debt in my opinion would be considered debt for things such as the latest tv entertainment systems, personal vehicles, tech gadgets, the latest iPad, or iPhone and things of this nature; basically, items which are not going to make any money.

If you buy a car for personal use, as soon as you drive out of that car yard, the car depreciates in value instantly. So if you already have a car which is getting you from A to B, then ask yourself is upgrading to the latest model really necessary and if it can possibly wait until you get into a better position with larger debts like the mortgage?

Having the latest gadgets is another cost that will not make you money and therefore in my opinion would be considered as a bad debt. Again, do you really need the newest, biggest 4k, 8k digital television with surround sound? Usually, you get items like this on store credit with a deal like no interest for 20 months, which sounds great. You hear interest free and immediately think you are beating the system. This is all part of the trap at keeping us where these financial institutions want us, paying lines of credit each week and crippling our cashflow which keeps us treading just above water month to month.

I am not saying we need to live a minimalist lifestyle and go back to the good old days of the Nokia 3310 with polyphonic ring tones; I am simply saying that we need to be mindful of these debts and not to get caught up using the line of credit for such items or bad debts. If we are, then we are not using the financial tool correctly, which will cause us more harm than good.

The large financial institutions have been feeding us information for years about credit cards, and our understanding is all wrong.

For instance, my younger sister is just entering the workforce and is looking to buy a car. I asked her about getting a credit card to implement this strategy to pay the car loan off within 12 months opposed to 5 years. Her response was that she was scared to get the credit card because she did not trust herself and her spending habits. This is far too common with people and because we have created this fear that a credit card is a bad thing, we tend to steer clear of ever owning one. I am happy to say that my sister implemented this strategy and she managed to pay off the vehicle loan completely in 6 months. A $10,000 loan was paid off completely in a fraction of the time, saving her a few thousand in interest payments to the bank.

When getting a new credit card, it's all about the rewards points and schemes they push which make us want to spend and rack up points to get these rewards. For every dollar we spend, we get 2 points! Yeh, let's go buy a new home entertainment system and get loads of points then we can get more things with the points. Spend on a family holiday to gain more points and shop on a daily basis. Spend! Spend! Spend! The more we spend the more we are rewarded. Our brains see the credit card rewards as a good thing and we want more and more.

Fact of the matter is that we need to spend hundreds of dollars, if not thousands, to get minimal back and the reward is nothing compared to what we are spending.

I spent four years investing in myself and trying my hand at trading in the forex market. I spent many hours studying, reading books and researching different strategies and the main focus was not on trading, but on controlling our behavior and our own psychology. It was through this experience I learned more about our association with money than ever before.

Trading is simple. Anyone can open an account, deposit money and then open a trade simply by the click of a button. The real challenge is mastering human psychology and behaviour, controlling our own impulses and disconnecting from the emotional value of money.

We, as humans, associate feelings when we win or lose money. We have emotional connection with money and that is because when we win money, we associate feelings like joy and happiness and our endorphins go crazy and we want more and more, just like playing the poker machines with all the flashing lights and catchy tunes when we get the feature spin. Some people have addictions to spending money on items which they don't really need. It's just the buzz of buying and getting the best deal.

I never did very well in trading forex as I could not control my emotions when I would win. I would start to over trade and step outside of my trading plan which inevitably would cost me my winnings and more. Once I would lose my money, then I would be angry with myself as I knew exactly what I did wrong and why I lost my money, but at the time my emotions took control and I would not be able to control this behavior. I even signed up and started to learn automated trading to take the emotions out of my trading, however it was 3 months after I signed up for the 12-month training course I was diagnosed and therefore could not continue.

On the other hand, when something is taken away, we associate feelings of sadness or anger. If you lose $100, you don't feel happy and say, 'oh well, some lucky person will have a good day when they find it'. We are angry to have lost our hard-earned money, as we just traded how many hours to make that $100? I was never one to play the pokies, or bet on horses, as I hated losing my money all the time, so I just stopped playing or betting on them out of anger. Unfortunately, this is not the case for many people, as there are many out there that will be paid on a Friday and sit at the pub on a Friday night, playing the dreaded machines until all their money is gone.

Using the line of credit tool incorrectly will almost always have a negative outcome for many of us, which means large debt we will struggle to pay.

This is where the financial institutions want us, and they keep us here by giving us loans that charge huge amounts of interest until we are struggling neck high in debt. They are just waiting for us to default on our loans and then take the lot! We are hearing more and more of that happening these days, due to the inflation of property in our major cities. People buying into the property market with low interest deals, then come the rate rise, people already struggling with debt are now defaulting on loans they simply could not afford from the beginning. Our friends at the banks will then reposes their homes and sell them so they get their money back.

Financial Tools

A line of credit or credit cards are not to be considered bad financial tools as if used correctly, they can save thousands. There is a saying here in Australia; 'a good tradesman never blames his tools'. We should not blame the banks but change our attitude and habits and prioritize our spending to utilize what they are offering in the right way. These tools will help us and work to our advantage in a big way and potentially save us thousands of dollars and get us to achieving our goal of owning our own home in much less time.

Summary

→ Good debt is something which has the potential to make us money, including our home

→ Bad debit is something which will not make us money

→ Limit bad debt

→ Change our attitude, habits, prioritize spending

→ Don't fear the line of credit or credit card it is a tool and can be used with great effect

→ Use the financial tools wisely and correctly

Chapter 7

Line vs Loans

Different Interest types (amortized and simple)

Not many people are aware of the different types of interest we are being charged from the large financial institutions. We don't understand the fine print details of the interest and how it is calculated, so we simply trust they are choosing the best for us, and we never question it.

I was one of those people and hadn't realized or paid attention to just how much was being taken from my pockets on a monthly basis. But now in my situation, having my life potentially cut very short and never seeing the day when I would pay off and fully own my home, I took notice! To be honest, once I noticed how much I was paying and giving away, I got really angry, and I knew it was time to make some changes. I am not a financial advisor, nor have I ever worked in the finance industry. I pay my taxes and work as hard as I can to earn my living and this is what many of us are doing daily. Through some of my own research I have discovered that these large financial institutions, depending on the product (or tools) we acquire from them, have two different types of interest which are applied to our loans and they are **Amortized or Simple Interest**.

Amortized Interest

For many of us, the dream of owning our own home is one that both motivates us and scares us at the same time. It motivates us to work hard to provide a safe haven for our family; to put a roof over our kids' heads. On the other hand, it's a scary thought to be locked into a huge loan for 30 years, paying ridiculous amounts of interest to the bank.

There are many different types of loans out there and, as I am not a mortgage advisor or financial advisor, I cannot comment on which types of loans are best suited for individuals.

When we go to the banks or the financial advisor, we trust that they will find us the best loan suited to our situation yet find ourselves locked into a loan product with usually either a fixed rate or a variable rate. If we get the standard principal and interest home loan, then our repayments will be paying off the principal (the amount we initially borrow) and interest (the amount we pay the banks for lending us the money).

There are other types of loans such as interest only loans, where the banks will lend us a sum of money and then we only pay back the interest each month and not the principal (usually taken out for investment properties to keep the payments low and keep money in our pockets). The issue with the interest only loan is that because we never pay the principal off then we will never own the asset and the banks will continue to make their profits each month. And remember, if the interest rates rise (they are at all-time lows here in Australia 2020, so the only way is up), we will pay more to the banks and if we cannot afford the rate rise, the banks will repossess the property.

These loans are the main product the banks push. The one I found they push the hardest is the fixed Principal & Interest home loan (P&I). With the fixed home loan there is a cap to the amount of additional money we can pay off the principal each year (usually $10,000), and if we pay more than this, we will be charged additional fees for paying off our home loan! So, we are penalized for paying off our own home loan quicker!

The reason behind getting us on the fixed rate is that the banks will then be able to get the most out of us in terms of the interest payments which we will be paying them each month and due to the fact we cannot pay more than $10,000 off the principal per year, they are guaranteeing their profits and keeping us right where they want us.

On the variable loan, we can pay as much additional monies off the principal as we can afford but usually the rate for this loan is a little higher than the fixed rate. Most of us will see the smaller fixed rate and as its smaller we opt for this option with no hesitation as the repayments each month will be slightly smaller as well. Sounds like a no brainer, right? Well until now anyway, as our mindset and attitude are changing.

What we did was to split our homeloan part fixed and part variable. We calculated roughly how much additional payments we were aiming to make within the fixed period and we left this figure on the variable loan and the larger portion was fixed.

All these types of loans (and others such as car loans, student loans) have what is called Amortized interest. Amortization is the process of spreading out a loan into a series of fixed payments over time. You'll be paying off the loan's interest and principal in different amounts each month, although your total payment to the financial institution remains equal each period. The amortized interest is a calculated over the entire figure which we borrow and even though the rates are usually smaller and now in Australia (the lowest they have been in many years), we are paying large amounts of interest to the bank each month from our monthly payment. The reason for this is the fact that the banks make us pay back the interest first before we pay off our principal. This is ensuring they will get all their money before we pay off our homes.

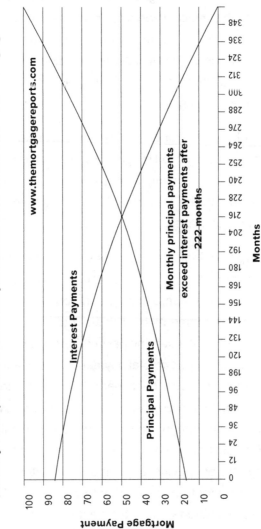

See loan amortization chart above Graph 7.1 – showing in the beginning of the amortized loan, over 80% of our fixed payment is interest, which goes directly to the bank.

If you take a good look at your mortgage or loan documents, you will notice that if you are to carry on and pay this set monthly fee for the life of the loan then you will be paying back to the big bank almost double what you borrowed! Yes, that is correct. You will pay almost double what you borrowed, if not more than double. For example, my wife and I originally borrowed $881,176 and would pay back $1,570,581.48 if we paid back the loan as per the amortized schedule. This was what I had been doing, as I was never shown anything different.

I put it to you in a different way.

Ask yourself this question, 'would I be happy to pay a stranger $1,500 a month for nothing?'

Of course, the answer is a big fat NO!

Then why are we happy to do this with the huge financial institutions on a monthly basis? And the answer is because we are never shown any other way around it and we accept the fact if we have a mortgage then we owe the banks their interest and we simply carry on paying them, no questions asked.

By using these tools correctly, we are able to leverage our money against the bank and to our benefit. For instance, if we had a cashflow of $500 each month some might say well why not just put this $500 onto the mortgage and save all the headache of setting up new accounts and getting lines of credit only to pay the same debt? The difference with this is that instead of handing over our $500 to the bank, which we would then lose or have to take from the re-draw if we needed it back, we use **their money** to **pay our loan** and we are transferring debt from an amortized interest loan to a simple interest loan, saving us large amounts of interest and cutting time off the loan.

The Amortized Calculator

I have come across a web site which I have found to be fairly accurate when it comes to calculating the amortized rates and payments for my loans. I simply found this through a google search and this is the one I personally used.

https://www.calculatestuff.com/financial/loan-amortization-calculator

For example, we can simply put in our individual figures of the loan amount $450,000, interest rate 3.42% and the term left on the loan say 30 years. This calculator will show us a breakdown of the years left to pay, the total amount payable to the bank, the main balance each year, how much our re-payments will be each month / year, calculate how much interest we pay each month / year and then showing the all-important figure of how much principal we are actually knocking off with each month / years payments.

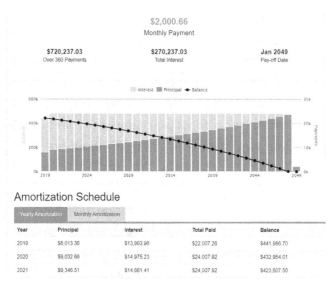

Amortization Schedule

Year	Principal	Interest	Total Paid	Balance
2019	$8,013.30	$13,993.96	$22,007.26	$441,986.70
2020	$9,032.69	$14,975.23	$24,007.92	$432,954.01
2021	$9,346.51	$14,661.41	$24,007.92	$423,607.50

Above is an example only

Graph 7.2

From here we can then see that to pay off approximately $9,000 principal we would have to pay approximately $15,000 in interest with a total out of pocket cost for the year $24,000. Therefore, if we are able to pay say $9,000 lump sum off the principal then we would be saving $15,000 instantly and this money will stay in our pocket. By transferring $9,000 to a simple interest loan we would only be paying approximately $157 in interest per month on a 21% interest rate credit card. Yet we just saved $15,000 instantly by making the lump sum payment.

Simple Interest

Simple interest is a form of interest which is an annual rate, calculated daily and charged monthly. The simple interest is used on tools such as the everyday Credit Card and another product which the banks have to offer which you may not know anything about are Home Equity Lines of Credit (LOC).

There are many different credit cards on the market, and they all have different rewards, fees and annual costs, so looking into these is a crucial step before making any commitments. Usually on the credit cards the interest rates for cash advances are around 21% per annum (calculated daily and charged monthly), if you shop around you can find better rates and is another reason you will need to do your own homework to best suit your individual needs.

You may see this interest rate and straight away think this is so much higher that your existing home loan of 3.42%, however the catch is that just because this rate is higher, it's not necessarily worse.

Simple interest is just a different unit which is calculated daily and charged monthly on the amount left outstanding in the account at this time.

Due to the way it is calculated, and the total amount of the loan is far less than the mortgage, the interest charged will be far less than that charged on the amortized mortgage loan. By using these tools, we will be able to use the banks money to put lump sum payments onto our mortgage, saving us thousands of dollars.

Line of Credit

A LOC is a revolving source of money, meaning we can continually take money out as long as we are putting money in. The LOC is a tool which the banks have on offer, but we simply are not taught to use this in the correct way. A LOC simply means that once we put money back onto the line, we can take this right back out if needed. Depending on your circumstance there are two options for getting a LOC.

Option 1 – A Home Equity Line of Credit (my opinion best option and what I have set up)

Depending on your existing financial lender, they will have different names for this type of loan. These types of loans are commonly secured to the existing mortgage to your property therefore you would need to have a little equity in your home to qualify for this type of product. The minimum amount is around is $20,000.

All the different lenders have different set fees, rates and terms for their products, therefore it is important to look at these and consider if they will be best suited to your situation and if needed to speak with a separate, independent financial advisor to assist you in making your decision.

We had set up the line of credit directly through the bank instead of using the credit card. We had enough equity in our property, so we saw this as the best option for us at the time. We are currently paying $395 per year for the home loan package which means we did not pay additional fees for the Line of Credit (LOC). We were able to get a discounted interest rate and no annual fees for the LOC. Therefore, it made this process very straight forward and was opened within one week. Once the LOC was opened, we made our first bulk payment of $20,000 onto our home loan! I knocked my principal down by $20,000 in an instant and saving a whopping $38,000 in interest payments and cut years off my loan term, all by using the banks money. We simply transferred $20,000 from an amortized loan to a simple interest loan.

Limit type	Limit	Start	Balance	Debit interest rate
Overdraft	$20,000.00	01/05/2019	$0 to $20,000	4.79% p.a
		For balances over this approved limit, the debit excess interest rate of 17.94% p.a. applies		

Taxes & interest	This accrual period	2018-19 financial year	2019-20 financial year
Loan interest	$29.50 DR	$7.08 DR	$77.80 DR

Graph 7.3

The above Graph 7.3 is a snippet from my online banking to show just how much interest I paid on this $20,000 bulk payment. (Remember the size of this bulk payment is relative to my wife and I cashflow situation with the aim on getting this paid down in 6 months). This snip was taken in August 2019 which we still have some to pay off, but you can see just how little ($77.80) the interest *is on the LOC opposed to the amortized interest loans ($1,918.12) per month.*

However, please be aware of the below regarding bulk payments/bank transactions over $10,000.

Also one thing to note is that there are three main activities which require banks to interact regularly with the Australian Transaction Reports and Analysis Center (AUSTRAC) the first being they have an obligation to report all suspicious activity, Second is any transaction over $10,000 is to be reported, being physical cash, and electronic funds transfers and the third the banks must report all international funds transfers irrespective of the amount.

AUSTRAC operates as a dual regulator and is responsible for the administration and enforcement of the Anti-money Laundering and Counter Terrorism Financing Act 2006 (Cth) (AML/CTF Act)

(Above quoted from Banking and Lending Practices Fifth edition)

Option 2 – Credit Cards (remember it's a tool)

As I mentioned previously, the credit card option is one many people will struggle to see the benefit of and will most likely be deterred by the fees which they think will be much higher. Most Credit Card fees for money transfers are around the 21% mark and will have a cash advance fee around 2-3%. In my experience I took $4,893.10 from my Credit Card and was charged $3 for the cash advance fee, not to mention that this $4,893.10 payment instantly saved me around $8,000 of interest payments to the bank. So, $8,000 staying in my pocket not there's.

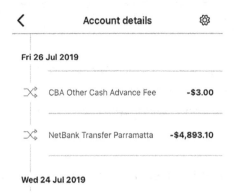

Credit Card Account Graph 7.4
showing the fee for the cash advance.

Just because the credit card has a higher interest rate this does not mean it is worse than the smaller rate on the amortized loan. This lump sum payment will automatically save you more than your offset account, also enabling you to leverage your money against the bank and not just hand it over. By using a LOC or revolving source of money like a credit card, then if there was an emergency and we needed funds, it would be easily accessible and not affect the home loan amount.

The Oh So Great Re-Draw Facility

Here in Australia, we can have what is called a Redraw facility linked to our loans (depending on our lenders and product which we have from them) which is basically when we pay additional funds onto the loan, the monies accumulate and we are able to access these monies at any time for our own use primarily to upgrade our homes or assets. Our monthly payment is automatically adjusted, and we continue to pay our loan as usual. Its sits there in our account inciting us to use it, and many people do this for many different reasons which may not always be a bad thing. If the monies are going towards a good debt which will help accumulate an income producing asset (like renovating your home to increase the overall value), then this is not such a bad thing, right?

Before accessing the Redraw, remember just how long it took you to pay down the principal and how much interest you have paid the big financial institutions to get to this point. In our previous example, we paid a total to $24,000 to the bank which $15,000 was interest and only $9,000 off the principal. For every $9,000 we take from the Re-Draw, we will have to pay back $15,000 in interest to get back to the same point. By using this Redraw, it sets us back thousands of dollars and is what the banks want us to do so they keep us paying them huge amounts of interest payments which are all profit for these institutions!

Weigh this up, and if it is still viable, utilize this facility. Each situation and circumstances will be different, so before making any decisions about redrawing monies, please do your research and due diligence, or this will take you right back to where you began.

Could smaller amounts be borrowed directly from the LOC which means you would not be paying large amounts of interest to the banks?

Can it wait a little longer until the home is paid off and you have an investment property which would bring tax benefits and income?

There are options available, you just need to do your homework and decide what best suits your personal situation.

The Offset Account

In Australia, we have the offset accounts which are accounts linked to an existing or new home or investment loan. The way they work is that the money you have in these accounts will offset the amount you owe on the home or investment loan, and you will only be charged the interest on the difference. For instance, if you owe $450,000 but you had $50,000 in your offset then you would only be charged interest on $400,000.

What I found is that the amount of interest saved on these types of accounts is very minimal, and banks usually charge around $400 per annum for this product as part of a package (I pay annually $395), and yet these banks will push us to take out as many offset accounts as possible.

I have never had large amounts of 'spare' money sitting in my account; therefore, the saving is minimal. Over the course of 12 months I only saved $1,500. I'm not saying they are a bad thing, as every penny saved in our pocket is worth it. What I am saying is that we should not rely on this tool as our only vehicle for saving on interest, as we can save much more by implementing a simple strategy which will get results instantly. As I said earlier, a lump sum payment onto the loan can save us up to $15,000 depending on the size of the lump sum. I found usually whatever the lump sum is, it equates to nearly double in savings on the interest, so even $1,000 lump sum payment would save nearly $2,000 in interest payments. Already better than the offset account, it's not even using your own money. It is using the banks tools and money.

I would challenge anyone to check their individual figures against the amortized schedule and then see what you can be saving by using this method of the lump sum payment. It will soon become apparent that by using a LOC or credit card, the benefits will far outweigh the negatives and will save more money than simply relying on the offset accounts for savings.

Before making any decisions on this information, you should first consider if these items are appropriate to your circumstances and possibly seek professional advice specific to your needs, including financial, taxation and legal advice.

Summary

→   Do your own research and educate yourself (it's painful but empowering)

→   Know your individual lenders fees and conditions before applying yourself

→   Understand the tools available and use them correctly according to your individual circumstances

→   Smaller is not always better in terms of interest rates

→   Start small and see how it works, remember look at the compound effects not the one-off transaction

→   Only take bulk payment relative to your ability to pay back the line of credit in a timely manner (3-6 months tops), the more bulk payments we can put down per year the better

→   LOC are revolving source of money so you always will have access to this money in an emergency

→   Use the funds for good debt not bad debt

Chapter 8

6-12 months to live

Important steps to change

Since the Esophagectomy on the 1st of May 2019, I have been in recovery mode, trying to get used to life after surgery minus my stomach and esophagus. I was at home recovering and around the four week mark post op when I began to have major stomach pains which led to vomiting attacks that would last around 10-12 hours. During these attacks, I would be curled up on the bathroom floor, crying in pain and vomiting so hard it felt like my head was going to explode, all the while my wife would be standing there watching me helplessly. At my six week post op checkup following the Esophagectomy, I went in to see the surgeon to have the feeding tube removed from my stomach, and it was at this point the surgeon broke the news that the cancer had spread to my liver, lymph nodes in my neck and stomach. I asked the Doctor what this meant, and his response to me was,

'Michael you will die of Esophageal cancer and it will not be long.'

He gave me 6-12 months to live.

My wife and I walked out of there in silence, collected our daughter from day care and drove home heartbroken and distressed.

We had to re-assess our situation again.

Dealing with something like this, especially with a young daughter, is difficult on so many levels and it affects everyone around you in different ways. You would be surprised just how aware my four-year-old daughter is of the situation and her surroundings. Because she has been coming in and out of the hospitals with me, seeing me in intensive care unit, needles, tubes and everything hanging out of her Daddy, there has been nights when I am putting her to bed she says things like, 'when will the doctors fix you and get rid of the lump?'

(We don't use the C word we call it the lump).

She asks if she is going to catch my lump and get sick as she doesn't want to get needles.

'Why can't they fix you?'

The most upsetting thing for me is when she tells me she is scared and upset that I am sick. There have been nights when I lay there with her and just cry when she is sleeping.

I lost my father when I was only four years old, and I think due to this, the thought of death does not scare me. I have always said growing up that I would be here for a good time not a long time and once I die, I will be able to catch up with my father and finally get the chance to sit chat and enjoy the small things which I was never able to do.

This might sound silly to some. I guess this is my way of dealing with the situation and finding comfort in the unknown. For me at the moment, the hardest thing I struggle with is knowing through my actions, or lack of, if I was to die in the next 6-12 months, then my legacy to my family will be large debt and really is the one thing that hurts the most. Yes, my wife and I could have had better insurances in place to help minimize the effects of an early unexpected death, but still it would be nice to be freed of the stress and pressure of the financial burden sooner rather than later, and not having to rely on the motivation of a medical disaster to pay off our home.

My wife has a whole different range of emotions which she is dealing with on a daily basis and it is something that I cannot control, nor can I say everything will be ok. It is very difficult to sit by and watch my loved ones go through emotions like anxiety, panic attacks and depression, all because of what is happening to me and our uncertain future.

Sometimes, I wish this was over and I would be dead to ease this pain, however this is not fair to our beautiful daughter who deserves her parents for as long as she needs us. To my wife's credit, she has shown again and again just how incredibly strong and resilient she is. Through this whole process, she has managed to continue to get out of bed, going about her daily routine, to work full time, to look after our daughter and support me as my wife.

The fact is that when we die, our loved ones are the ones who will have to work, look after our kids, and this also means pay the bills, mortgage, living expenses, schooling and more, all while grieving for the loss of a loved one.

Knowing that through my ignorance (not prioritizing my health and insurances), I would be adding to the stress and pressure of the situation, as well as still having a large mortgage to pay, there is the added fear of not knowing what the future will bring. Worrying if my wife will have to sell the house, move elsewhere and start from scratch, as she is not originally from Australia, with none of her immediate family around, and being here all alone amplifies this feeling of fear and uncertainty.

I think in this day and age we sometimes take for granted the little things in life which are right in front of us, like our family or our health, all because of the pressures we are dealing on a daily basis and a big factor is the financial burden we all carry.

Now, more than ever, something must change.

We found this strategy which enabled us to re-set our thinking and which gave us hope and a purpose to keep going with something to focus our energy towards. In the beginning, my wife and I made a few simple changes which had a profound impact, not only mentally, but also seeing the results instantly was a great motivator to keep going.

Setting up Terminal Velocity in 10 easy steps

Making changes to enable this strategy was simpler than I imagined.

The steps to change began with:

1. Changing attitude and realizing there is something we can do to make a difference

2. Creating the budget and spreadsheet

3. Confirming our cashflow for the month

4. Opening up the everyday spending account

5. Opening up a Line of Credit (either credit card or home equity line of credit)

6. Setting up regular transfer for wages to go into the line of credit

7. Setting up regular transaction for the daily spending to be sent from the LOC to daily spending account

8. Changing bills to be taken from the LOC at the end of the month (this enables us to minimize the interest we will be paying on the LOC ad maximize savings)

9. Track spending and expenses as they come in confirming on our budget spreadsheet

10. Make lump sum payment once the LOC is paid back to nil

Attitude Adjustment

We needed to change our attitude towards our money and the perception that we need to exchange time for money, instead making our money work for us.

This means leveraging our money against the banks and not being happy to simply hand over our money each month and paying huge amounts of interest. By using the tools available through lines of credit, we can start to make our money work for us.

By starting small and giving ourselves time to adjust and fine tune our budget, expenses and cashflow, this gave us confidence that change is not a bad thing. Lines of Credit are not a bad thing and we can actually make a difference and pay down our debts faster, saving money in the process.

At the beginning of our journey, many people would ask me, 'what was the point of opening and using the LOC to make these payments? I can just save my own money and make these payments, or I just pay more each month.'

My answer to this is simple.

By leveraging the **banks money** against themselves, we are simply transferring a lump sum figure to a simple interest loan rather than the amortized interest. It saves us money instantly.

We don't have to blindly hand over our hard earned money as the lines of credit are a fluid source of money. We can make a bulk payment instantly and not have to spend months saving up (all whilst paying interest each month) and simply handing it all over. If we need access to money for an emergency, we can simply draw on this LOC and not the Redraw facility, which will mean we would be paying large amounts of interest to the bank just to get back to where we began.

During my cancer diagnosis there has been a few months were expenses have been more than expected, therefore my wife and I were able to use the LOC to pay off the medical bills (not effecting our home loan) and simply carry on paying down the LOC all whilst paying minimal interest to the bank. Over the course of 6 months we have only paid $141.51 in interest and have paid $36,000 off the principal saving approximately a whopping $72,000 in interest payments.

Graph 8.1

above is a snip from our bank account in September showing when we opened up the LOC (May) and made the first transaction. You can see in our situation from May to September we have only paid the bank $109.23 in interest and paid thousands off our principal.

By using the banks money, we do not have to spend months saving up our own money, all whilst paying interest to the bank. We see instant results and our mortgage is being paid off. This is a great feeling and keeps us focused.

By seeing these instant results, it really made us feel great and that we were now actually achieving something together and something of great importance in our lives. Even though I may only have six months to live, it is the start of something great. This is something that my wife will continue to do in the event that my doctors are right and this gives my wife hope and me a sense of relief that my family may be able to cope with our debt once I am gone.

Limit type	Limit	Start	Balance	Debit interest rate
Overdraft	$20,000.00	01/05/2019	$0 to $20,000	4.73% p.a.
		For balances over this approved limit, the debit excess interest rate of 17.94% p.a. applies		

Taxes & interest	This accrual period ⓘ	2018-19 financial year	2019-20 financial year
Loan interest	$20.59 DR	$7.08 DR	$141.51 DR

Graph 8.3
Above taken in October we have paid
$36k off the principal and only paid $141.51 in
interest on the LOC

Summary

→ Change our attitude and understand the importance of the cashflow

→ Get our money working for us

→ Stay focused and on track once we start making the bulk payments

Chapter 9

Owning our situation

Continuing to create income through property

Since having a time limit put on my life, it makes me look back at the decisions I have made throughout my life and in doing so, it also makes one realize just how much we as humans have become more like robots. We follow the crowd, too afraid to question why we do what we do, and too afraid to ask if there are better options available to us. We have become so trusting, and simply except what we are told from these so-called experts like doctors, dietitians and the banks.

When it comes to my financial situation, up until this diagnosis, I was following the crowd, doing what I was told and simply playing along by their rules which looking back now has really got me nowhere. It took me until I was handed down a cancer diagnosis to stop, reassess, take control and own my personal finance situation.

I have always been a firm believer that investing in bricks and mortar (property) is the best way to go, as this is a physical object and not just numbers on a screen (stock market).

For me investing in property was a better option rather than giving our monies to these investment / super funds, as I felt more in control. Investing in stocks can be a lucrative venture, however instead of blindly handing over our money to strangers why not educate ourselves and take the responsibility to invest our own money on stocks we choose. In my opinion giving our money blindly to these companies was more of a risk therefore I opted to invest in property. Investing in housing is physical and will always be something that will be required by somebody, somewhere, no matter where you are in the world.

At the time of my diagnosis, my super was a measly $24,000 and I had been working since I finished school at 18 years of age. I have been in a trade and technically been a sole trader and should have been putting my money towards my superannuation. I worked hard, saved my monies and invested in property, only to be doing it all wrong because I was never given another option or was being sold information that was not best suited to my situation.

Once we got the investment property and started paying for this new mortgage and bills, with the rent coming in we still had to pay around $500 per month towards this property. If anything changed, say the property was vacant or interest rates increased, we would be in financial hardship, as we are already at maximum capacity with our own personal loan.

Looking back now, I feel that our best option would have been not to jump straight into this new investment loan, but rather pay off our personal mortgage first, before committing to another large loan. Then, we would not have found ourselves in over $1.2m worth of debt.

The best possible situation would have been to pay down our own personal debt to either zero (meaning not investing for a few years) or at least to a point where we could actually afford to pay the mortgage on the investment loan, especially if circumstances changed. To have our personal mortgage paid off completely would mean that our monthly cashflow would be around $9,000 as there is no large debt hanging over our heads and all this money can be used to pay down an investment property in a fraction of the 30 year loan term. By combining our cashflow and the rental income, this would be over $10,000 per month and using the LOC to pay large chunks onto the loan, this mortgage could be paid down in no time at all. Seriously, we could have be paying an additional $120,000 off the principal per year.

However, we are in this situation where we have an investment property and our large home loan, therefore we cannot afford to pay additional monies off this investment property and currently the rent does not cover all the mortgage repayments. Our money is not working for us and we are creating more stress and unwanted pressure.

After leaving the investment loan on Principal and interest (P&I) for 6 months, we have now changed our investment loan to interest only (IO) for a 12-month period to reduce the mortgage and ensure the rent covers the bills. This will make sure what little money we saved up will cover the bills for the next 12 months. The downside to going onto IO type loan is we will never be able to get in front, as all we do is pay the banks their interest and never knock down the principal. The banks are the only winners in this scenario. Yes, the repayments are lower, and the rent will cover the repayments, however we are never closer to owning this property and making our money work for us.

Before changing to IO, I calculated that we would only be paying off around $7k in principal being on a P&I type loan, so to make my money work for me, I will now use the LOC to pay this $7k ensuring we are still paying this loan down and that our repayments don't increase at the end of the interest only term. The beauty is that I will be using the banks money to pay the principal down whilst the rent pays the interest.

Because we have invested into this new property a lot sooner than we should have, paying this down will take that little bit longer as we are juggling between our home and the investment property. However, once this is paid down and the rent is covering the mortgage, the additional monies will be used to increase our monthly cashflow and help pay down the line of credit faster enabling us to pay lump sum payments quicker.

Debt Free – Now What?

Once we become mortgage free from our own home and the investment property, we will be able to increase the LOC to enable us to purchase another property, however this time all the cashflow and rent can be used monthly to pay down the line of credit and pay larger lump sums quicker. By doing this, we are going to generate a source of income for ourselves and a source of income which nobody can take from us, because we will own these properties and not the banks. Over time, if we were able to purchase a number of properties and completely pay them off each month, the rent will become our income or retirement money for the future, not to mention if we do our due diligence and invest in the right places at the right time we can also make money through the capital growth of the properties. Our long term goal is to keep the properties as the rental is a source of income we are not looking to buy and sell, as we want to be able to stop trading time for money, remember?

There are many ways to invest in property and many different strategies, so for this reason it is always good to do your own homework, know the market, speak to professionals and get advice before signing your life away and buy into property. Making informed decisions is crucial but it's also about our attitude to how we pay them off and get them working for us!

Our Health Is Our Most Important Asset

When it comes to the health side of things, from the beginning I was very trusting of my doctors, surgeons and Oncologists. My local GP in the beginning sent me for the Endoscopy and Colonoscopy, and if it was not for her, I would not have discovered this disease as early as I did. However, I have come to realize that her actions or attitude to request this type of scans are somewhat rare as other doctors do not seem to act in the same way. I do have more faith in my local GP than some of these other doctors, such as oncologists and surgeons that I have come to meet. Speaking with other people about their personal experiences reiterates my feelings of distrust.

Not long after my diagnosis, a very close and dear friend was at home working when all of a sudden, he got up to get some water and had severe chest pains, fell to his knees and passed out, wetting his pants in the process. When he came to, he managed to get himself to the bathroom and call his wife who arranged for the neighbor to come and take him to the local GP where he passed out again in the waiting room, wet his pant again and woke up in the doctors room! The doctor simply gave him a prescription for some medication and sent him on his way. After hearing this I was angry at his GP, and insisted he go find another GP as this could not be something to be taken lightly. Look at me for example. I had no symptoms and yet I have been given 6-12 months to live! To cut a long story short, he did find another doctor who carried out many tests and scans that came back negative. Even though the test came back negative, at least he was able to tick these off the list and be confident there was nothing more sinister going on inside.

From the day I was diagnosed, and because I had not been faced with anything like this before, I was very trusting of the doctors who were treating me. Over the course of the coming months, I became a lot more skeptical and not so trusting. I instantly thought that doctors have my best interest at heart and would be doing everything in their power to ensure I am given the best chance to beat this or any disease that I am dealing with. They are the ones that have been through many years of schooling, learning and treating others, therefore their opinion or treatment options must be the best, right?

From my personal experience, I can see how different one's journey can be if we are too afraid to take control of our personal situation and really change our attitude towards our health.

With the doctors, I have found that not always are they giving me the full or right information. I was diagnosed on a Thursday and the following Thursday I met with the Oncologist who had already booked me in for a surgery to have the central line (PICC Line) installed in my arm in preparation for the first lot of chemotherapy. I did not question this central line and accepted that it must go in my arm and this was the best option. Later, after discussing this with a friend who was going through bowel cancer, he mentioned he had a central line installed under his skin in his chest (Porta-Cath), meant he did not have any open wounds on his body. I did not question this as I did not realize the implications of having chemo and an open wound. It was only when I ended up in the emergency ward twice when the central lines became infected, and caused a 5cm blood clot in my arm which then needed treatment and in the end delayed surgery for six weeks because of the infection and blood clot, that I started to think more about it.

Everything happened so quick in the first week after the diagnosis; seeing different doctors, surgeons and still coming to terms with what was happening. When I asked the Oncologist what my options were, he was adamant that I needed to act fast as time was of the essence. The early detection meant that I could have four bouts of chemo, surgery to cut out the tumor and then another four bouts of chemo and I would be cured! Then suddenly (or so it seemed) I found myself sitting in the chemotherapy chair halfway through my first course of chemo when the nurse asked me if I had spoken with the Oncologist about contraception during chemo. My reply was, 'no, nobody has spoken about anything like this. What is the problem?' At that she was shocked and a little uncomfortable in telling me that I should have been given the option to freeze my sperm, as chemo can make me sterile! I was shocked but accepted the fact that I needed to act fast and start chemo asap.

My wife and I started to do our own research into many different things, even simple things like taking natural supplements such as turmeric or super foods such as soursop tea, or other natural foods high in anti-oxidants which are supposed to help fight against cancer. The Oncologist told me to stay away from them as they could counteract the chemo. It was at this point I started to become a little skeptical, however I trusted the doctor, so I stayed clear of these foods. For the first four bouts of the chemo, I followed the doctor's instructions and put my trust in them. It was after the surgery that my attitude towards these doctors really changed.

I had been through the first four bouts of chemo and had the major operation to remove the original tumor and was expected to commence with another four bouts of chemo to get rid of any 'residual cancer cells' (these were the doctors words), however I kept asking the doctors if I needed to get more scans before starting the next lot of chemo until I finally got the referral to have a PET scan which came back with devastating results.

It was when I went back to the surgeon for the six week checkup that he broke the news of the new prognosis, and advised me to leave in my feeding tube which I had coming out of my bowel, as he said it would be in my best interest as the outlook was not good. I kindly refused and told him to remove this tube from my body as this would be one less foreign object my body would have to fight, and not to mention the threat of infection. Trying to keep it clean was a nightmare. On one occasion, the end of this tube fell out and my daughter noticed my internal fluids literally dripping out onto the floor!

It was after my second episode of the severe abdominal pains that my wife informed the surgeon she thought I had a bowel obstruction. The response from the surgeon was that I was too impatient, and all my plumbing had been re-arranged, therefore it would take time to get used to it, so 'go home and relax, take some medication and be patient'. I was dismissed and sent home with Buscopan and nausea tablets!!

It was only four weeks later that I was rushed in for emergency surgery to have the obstructed bowel fixed.

When I went to see the oncologist, following the devastating news of having 6-12 months to live, I asked what all my options are.

I stressed ALL my options.

I was told that I had two options; having another bout of chemotherapy, which was not as good as the first one, or going on an immunotherapy trial which had only been tested on 20 people worldwide and that was it! I even asked the Oncologist about taking CDB oil, (cannabis oil) but as he did not know anything about this, he did not comment. Again, I put my trust in the doctor. My wife, daughter and I left the office in shock, disbelief and again questioning how we got to this point.

The trial was meant to be for three months.

This could potentially be half of the rest of my life and was a big gamble as this drug was simply a trial. Not even the doctor knew if it would work.

My wife and I spoke with others about our story. We were chatting with friends from Israel who put us in touch with the cancer clinic at the Sheba Medical Centre. They asked me for test results from the tumor which the doctors here in Australia would have taken. When I asked my doctors for the test results, what I discovered next made me very angry and cast even more doubt over my treatment. They did not carry out all these tests!

This made me question how they decided that going on this trial for three months was the best thing for me? The doctors keep telling me everyone's cancer mutates differently, however they were giving us a blanket treatment; one size fits all!

I confronted the Oncologist and told him that I felt he was potentially wasting half the rest of my life for his own medical benefit for this study. I had also found out, by speaking with another oncologist, that there is a gene test which can be done which will be the most comprehensive test carried out on the tumor and would confirm if there was any specific drug on the market which could help treat my tumors. (The test is called Foundation One Genetic Testing). The doctors mentioned they were going to offer this test if the immunotherapy failed.

After three months, I had another scan and at this point it confirmed that the tumors had grown, and the immunotherapy trial has not worked. I was taken off trial. Three months of my potential six months gone because I trusted these doctors.

Again, I found myself in the Oncologist office discussing my next options. I requested the Foundation One test at this point (at my own cost of $6,000) and would then have to wait for the results. The Oncologist insisted I start treatment again, going on chemotherapy, the one which was not meant to be as good as the first regimen. My wife and I left there again feeling down. It was another setback, but after stopping for a minute and really thinking what was going on, I decided to take control and not to take up the offer of chemotherapy.

I mean, at this point I was eating better, feeling better, starting to exercise again (really lightly but still exercise), getting energy back and being able to play with my daughter, so to go back on chemo and poisoning my body all for the hope that it might work just did not make sense to me. I asked the doctor what the chances of it even working was, and his reply was that studies show it would be a 20-30% chance. The same doctor told me the first regimen of treatment was supposed to be a 50% chance, and look where I was now?

So, no thank you, Doctor!

I went home and started taking alternative treatments like Vitamin B17 (Apricot Kernels), CDB oils, vitamins for my liver, digestive system, eating fresh foods and really looking to build up my immune system by getting in fresh organic foods. For the next five weeks while I waited for the Foundation One Test to come back, I was feeling great. I was back working three days a week and looking after my daughter the other two days a week. I can guarantee I would not be doing this if I accepted the doctors offer of chemotherapy!

I received a call from the Oncologist's receptionist on a Wednesday confirming that I had treatment booked in on the Friday. I kindly declined this. Without even giving me the results of the test, the doctor simply booked me in to be hooked up and receive more drugs before even consulting me or my wife about our options!

I don't think so. I told the receptionist that I need to speak with the doctor first before I would be taking any of his drugs. She said she would get back to me shortly after speaking with the Oncologist. The next day, I received a call from the Oncologist himself, who gave me the results of the test over the phone. The results came back positive. In fact, they have identified a few drugs which might be able to assist in slowing down the tumors or better yet get rid of them.

I agreed to accept his drugs, but for the following week instead, which allowed us time to arrange an appointment to go through my report and the test results (which I insisted he email me the copy). After going through the report, my wife noticed there were a few other drugs on the list which had been identified that could possibly help my situation, therefore this was even more reason to sit down with the doctor and discuss my options as he never made me aware of these in the first instance.

A few months back, my wife came across an article from the UK about studies carried out in breast cancer patients with HERR 2 Positive Gene Mutation. Studies found that when two specific drugs were combined, in some cases tumors were disappearing in as little as 11 days!! Both these drugs were on my report; however, I was only offered the drug which would be for fee.

When we spoke with the Oncologist, we asked why the second drug was not originally offered if there had been positive results elsewhere in the world. The first response was that these would cost thousands of dollars, and then he stated that the test was carried out in breast cancer patients, and that there were no studies to either confirm or deny if this combination would be beneficial in treating Esophageal cancer.

If I would like to take it, I could.

The choice was mine.

Needless to say, I asked the doctor for a quote for this other drug which I will look to take if the newest drug I am on fails to make a difference.

I was fuming.

Who are these doctors to put a price tag on my life?

Just because something costs money does not mean this should not be offered to me. This is my life they are dealing with and they only offer the free option!

I have now come to the conclusion that I will not so easily trust the doctors and professionals when it comes to my health, and I must do *my own research into my own personal situation and challenge their opinions* as they might not always lay all the cards on the table and their option may not be the best one for my situation. We are all individuals and need to be treated as such and not treated as a collective cancer society because what works for me might not work for you!

Chapter 10

Things can always get worse

Attitude is Everything

My cancer diagnosis has profoundly altered the entire course and outlook of my life, not only physically, but also mentally. It's like looking around and being able to see life from a new perspective. I'm looking at the world through a new set of eyes. I was shocked at how little I was in control of my situation, and not prioritizing the important things in life, but also realizing how many others were in the same boat as me. They are just lucky they were not handed down a life changing diagnosis.

I soon realized that many of my friends and family did not have adequate or the best insurances in place to protect them or their families. They had the same arrogant attitude towards their health as I did, brushing aside aches and pains like its nothing to worry about. Slaving away to earn money, only to hand it all over to the banks like I was. They want to upgrade their homes by borrowing more, getting further in debt and not making their money work for them. Wanting the newest and best cars paying one off only to upgrade to the next model and simply, because they can.

These days, it's all so easy and available. Seeing how much people are afraid to own their situation, afraid of change, afraid of progress, set in their old ways just because that is what society has taught them, to be good little sheep and not question why we do what we do and to put all their trust in complete strangers angered me. It also inspired me to write this book in the hope that my journey could potentially change people's attitude towards their health, finances, life in general and ultimately take control of their situation.

Having a time limit put on your life really stops you in your tracks.

Time stands still, and it puts things into perspective instantly.

You start to question yourself and look back at what you have done with your life. How have I been as a husband, father, son, brother, friend? By looking back, I see that I have been going about life all wrong. It is something which is hard to admit, but also, I feel ashamed that it has taken something like this for me to recognize what I have right here in front of me every single day; my wife and beautiful daughter and the special people around me, who I have been taking for granted.

It's easy to get caught up in the rat race of life and my wife and I look back on years past and are amazed just how quickly the time had gone. Well, time never changes. It is just our perception of time and what we do to fill it in which makes it seem like it goes faster. A good friend of mine used to say, 'time is but an illusion', and this now makes more sense than ever. Every day we are on this earth, we are one day closer to the end of our lives. I have been told my end date could be 6-12 months. When will yours be?

For many years, my wife and I have been working hard to provide a decent life for ourselves and our daughter, which inevitably means we are always planning for the future, looking ahead and not looking at the now, today, this hour and minute. Ask yourself, 'What are you doing right now? Are you living in the moment?'

There were numerous times we argued about how much we were working, but we were prioritizing the wrong things, worrying about materialistic things and not the time with each other. Our attitude was all wrong. Then there was my arrogance and complacency towards my health, thinking something like this would never happen to me and making stupid comments like 'I am a god I will be fine' when my wife would ask me to go to the doctors or take notice of what my body was trying to tell me. At the time I thought I was being funny making light of these situations. Well, guess what? Turns out I am not a god after all!

Accepting our situation

The day we received the news, my wife and I had some really tough discussions about the potential outcome and as we didn't know the extent of the diagnosis, we were planning for the worst. Anything else would be a great result.

To have talks with my loved ones about the fact I might not make it to my daughter's next birthday, my wife's next birthday or Christmas was a really difficult thing to do, however if we shy away from these talks bury our head in the sand, then we are really just denying the reality of our situation. On the other hand, having these kinds of talks has helped us to acknowledge the facts, accept the situation and to move forward with life.

Acceptance of the situation is not easy, however for us to move forward and try to make sense and bring normality back to our lives, it has been a crucial part of the mental struggles. With accepting what is happening (not saying I'm happy about it!) and not burying my head in the sand denying what could potentially happen in the not so distant future, allows me to plan and make rational decisions to assist my family in the worst-case scenario.

For instance, I took my mother to the funeral directors to get a quote on my funeral and discuss things like what coffin I would like, if I would like to be buried or cremated, options for the ceremony etc. I did not have to do this, but if I chose not to think about this or discuss this, it would otherwise be left for others to deal with once I am gone. I know this was a hard thing for my mother to do, but it's something that is done now to help ease the pressure in the worst-case scenario. Not to mention, this was another insurance we could have had in place, however we don't, and my wife will be faced with a $16k bill for the funeral! By facing up to the reality of our situation, having these early discussions about the worst case scenario, we have been able to continue to move forward

When things go from bad to worse, it's not as shocking or we have become somewhat de-sensitized to the situation. I can assist while I am still here to help ease the burden of my loved ones and have some hope that in the event I am no longer around, my wife, daughter and family will be able to concentrate on each other to help one another through the grieving process.

By talking to others about our financial situation, it became apparent that I was not the only one who felt the same way towards the banks and being taken advantage of by these lending institutions. Yet, after speaking with so many, no one had the courage to implement change or was too afraid to try something new which could benefit them in so many ways.

Here and Now

We all have a time limit on our lives, but for the majority of us, we don't know when the end date will be. Ignorantly, we all assume it will not be until we are very old, and we never stop to think it could be in the next six months. Hell, it could be tomorrow for all we know (watch out for that bus heading your way).

Ask yourself; 'if you had a date to work to would you change the way you live, would you do things differently, would you act differently towards loved ones?'

On occasions, I remember just looking at my daughter, holding her and just really being present in that moment. Not speaking, just holding her and really being grateful for whatever time I will get to spend with her, here and now, not tomorrow or next week, but today, this minute, this second. If she would ask me to do something with her, before saying no I would ask myself why not? And most of the time, I would then make the effort to drag myself off the lounge and simply play and be there in the moment with her.

Before the diagnosis, there were many times my daughter would ask me to do something and I would give a pathetic excuse not to play with her like, 'Daddy's tired...had a stressful day at work...don't have time!' These were all excuses and just taking time with her for granted. Things like getting her ready for daycare, driving her there, picking her up, taking her to the park and all these little daily tasks that before the diagnosis could be stressful, all became much more important to me because who knew just how many times I would get to watch her play and grow? She does not need any of the latest and best gadgets. She does not need stupid amounts of toys. All she wants is her Daddy and Mummy to play with her and spend quality time with her. I was pushing her on the swing and sending messages for work on my phone.

She turned to me and said, 'get off that fucking phone before I throw it in the pool!'

She heard this from mummy apparently.

What more evidence do you need?

(I put the phone away before it went in the pool).

Because I lost my father when I was young, I know what it's like to grow up without a father. The anger of having him taken away from me at a young age was something I struggled to accept for many years. Our family did not talk about my father much, as losing your hero is difficult enough, but to talk about the past is not easy. All the raw emotions of that sad day would come back, making it feel like it was yesterday. I do not have any memories of my father, which adds to my pain and this is something that haunts me to this day, but in my situation I have decided to help the grieving process for my daughter in the event she also loses her father. I have opened an email account for my daughter, where I send through pictures of the random things we do, fun we have and write a little story for her to read when she is old enough. I found this to be a fun way to have her remember me.

Death is a certainty, and nothing can change that.

Looking at my daughter now, I draw great motivation to not give up for her. She did not ask to be born and it's our responsibility as parents to provide protection and guide her through life, until she is able to be an independent person. For this reason, I must focus on finding anything which could potentially help me prove the doctors wrong.

There are so many questions we can ask when faced with this type of situation. I think not letting ourselves get caught up asking the wrong questions is the key. I don't know what has caused this, neither do the doctors! They told me that for someone my age, fitness level, nonsmoker, light drinker (enjoying a wine or 2 with dinner every now and then) did not fit the bill at all and that it was just pure bad luck.

Asking questions like, 'why me...why us...what did I do to deserve this... how could this happen?' Questions like this can never be answered, and if we let our mind get caught up and ask ourselves these types of questions, dwelling on the past, then this will lead us down a dark and winding road, one which may lead to harm and self-destruction.

From the beginning, I have never been in that frame of mind. Instead, I have been asking what can we do to make this better? What can I do to help my body and mind? These types of questions motivate me to continue to fight this disease. I am not saying it's easy, because there have been very hard and difficult times and many of them. Now, I am having to watch my every action, feeling guilty when I do something which might not be good for me. Every decision I make, I now think about the consequences as I could be doing myself more harm and speeding up the potential outcome of this prognosis. My diet is my major focus as I have been reading many books and articles about natural healing and the one thing that keeps coming up is that diet is crucial to assisting the body to fight against cancer. Having chocolate or sweets comes with feelings of guilt, anger at myself for potentially letting my loved ones down, as I could be feeding the cancer.

It's a constant battle within my head, every day, every minute and every second.

There is no escaping it.

Then there are the feelings that I am becoming a burden to the people around me, causing them pain and suffering, having to watch me wilt away. There was a period where I lost around 14kg in 8 weeks due to the bowel obstruction and vomiting. At this point, when I looked in the mirror and saw the person looking back at me, it made me feel angry. This was not me, but there seemed to be nothing I could do to change this, nor could my loved ones for that matter, so dying might just be doing everyone a favor.

Because I was not leaving the house, I felt like I was losing my personality. I had nothing to talk about with family and friends, not making any jokes or laughing with people and becoming an empty soul, just waiting to die.

Another thing that I found difficult was the way this diagnosis affected others around me. Family don't know what to do or what to say. People that I have been friends with for many years tip toe around me, for fear of saying something wrong that would upset me in some way or another. Having to reassure people that I am still the same person they grew up with and came to know and love over the years just because I have this disease is exhausting. I have not changed inside, and I still like to laugh at the same things which have always made me laugh, just now my sense of humor is a little darker than before. There is nothing that anyone could say to offend me or upset me.

The fact is, this is something that is inside me now and there is no changing that, nor is there anything anyone can say or do to change that. No matter what is said and done, it is what it is. I don't know how many times a day I get asked how am I going? My answer is always, 'good!' But really, what am I expected to say? Everyone knows I would be feeling shit, having toxic drugs running through my body, killing every fast-growing cell, giving me all these side-effects that can only make me feel a certain way and it is far from good.

Trying to be strong and keep up a brave face to show others around you becomes tiring, and again is another daily struggle that we must deal with when faced with something like this. The easy option would be to sit inside, hide away, do what I am told by the medical experts and accept my fate. Or, I can stand up, question authority, not accept what I am told, educate myself, share my knowledge and experiences, trying alternative medications, eating right, exercising, meditating, opening my mind to alternative ideas and treatments use myself as a case study and be strong not only for myself but my loved ones around me, specially my daughter.

To my wife's credit, through this diagnosis she has been a true inspiration, my rock and confidant. Some days, I have been feeling down and depressed, tired and exhausted with having to put on the brave face day in day out, but she is always there to say the right things and to put things into perspective, even though she is going through all the same emotions and more.

Even though I have my wife, family and friends here with me, the cancer journey is a lonely one. All these feelings and emotions are going through my head, and no one around me can change the situation. It's something we need to fight ourselves and find strength within or in something to take our mind off the ever-present cancer battle. Even though we deal with these emotions within our head, I have found it beneficial to talk to others about the diagnosis, treatments, insurances, finances, my personal journey, sharing experiences, ideas and literature and by raising awareness I have come across many different people who have been through something similar. It becomes apparent that we are not alone and so many people out there are affected by the same things, day in and day out. By talking to others, I have learnt so much more about myself and my cancer journey and hopefully some of the knowledge I have gained can be beneficial to help so many others who might find themselves in a similar situation.

Once I came across the strategy, it became somewhat of an obsession. I had realized the potential to help myself and my family financially. By implementing changes to our attitude towards our personal health, changing the age old attitude of 'it will be right' or 'nothing to worry about', making changes to our finances and our spending habits, my wife and I have been able to regain control of our situation, empowering us to continue and to share our story with others, not only from a health perspective but also our financial journey as well.

Change can be a wonderful thing, so don't be scared to take the first steps and break free.

To my beautiful daughter Giulia,

For such a small girl you have an enormous personality. You have the ability to make me smile when things seem lost and just being in your presence makes me feel so privileged to be your father. You are so compassionate and caring towards others (even more so towards animals, just like your mother) it amazes me just how big your heart is, and I have learnt a thing or two from you over these past couple of years.

As you are a shy little girl, I always encourage you to be confident, and speak up using your 'loud voice' because I know just how special you are and how much you have to offer.

Be true to yourself and dream big. You have a wonderful imagination and can achieve anything you put your mind to. You always say you want to be a vet or a horse keeper (again showing your caring, compassionate side), and you can be these things if you are true to yourself and follow your dreams.

I always say to you 'knowledge is' and you reply 'POWER!'

I hope through educating yourself you will achieve your dreams, but also educate yourself through life (health, Insurances and finance) and life's experiences. I hope you will be able to chase your dreams with less of the stress and pressures which Mummy and Daddy had to go through.

Through this book, you will be able to see by having the right attitude, we can minimize the pressures of life. There is always another way to do something. Don't just rely on the first answer, take control of your situation and control your destiny.

If you can achieve financial freedom sooner rather than later, I hope this will give you more time chasing your dreams and the things which you are really passionate about. Enjoy every moment, no matter how small they may seem as this is what life is all about.

Having the right attitude through life is very important, as this is something that comes from within and something that only you as a person can change. There will be difficult times throughout your life, however it's how we deal with these situations and it's how we can stand up in the face of adversity and face our fears which define us as individuals.

You have the best role model right in front of you (Mummy). Throughout this whole diagnosis / prognosis, your mother has never stopped providing for us, nor has she succumbed to the gravity of the situation which is a true testament to her character and strength. This alone demands respect from those around her.

You are an inspiration to me, and therefore I will never give up.

I must remind myself that I am sick and it's upsetting to think that my time with you is limited. Daddy is scared to leave you and Mummy, but this is out of my control.

My main focus is getting better so I can be there for you. You are my inspiration and my life. I love you with all my heart and know you will make me and Mummy very proud. I will always be with you, no matter where you are in the world and I am so immensely proud of you as I know you will turn out to be a great strong woman just like Mummy.

I will be with you every step of the way.

I hope one day when you are older you can look back at the things I have done in life and the guidance I have given, and you can be proud of me.

I love you to the moon and back,

Daddy.

Acknowledgements

never thought in my wildest dreams I would ever write a book, nor did I ever think I would be diagnosed with a terminal disease!

Even though I have been dealt this card in life, this is not the end, in fact totally the opposite, I would not change anything. I have been granted a second chance to see all the important things I have around me in life, and the most important of all my friends and family, which have shown me just how special they are.

This book started out as an autobiography for my wife and daughter to have when I am gone, however after speaking with friends and family about the issues in this book (our financial situation and lack of insurances insurances) I realized I may be able to help so many more through sharing my personal story.

Firstly, to my beautiful **wife**, I have great admiration for your courage, strength and resilience. You are such an amazing person and an inspiration to me and our daughter. Throughout this journey there have been dark days however you have not missed a beat and continued to do what needs to be done for our family. I draw strength from the fact I have you by my side, I would only be half the man I am today without you. As we said on our wedding day ''Till death do us part''.

To my **Mum** (Annette Press), I would like to take this opportunity to say thank you! Our life journey has not been an easy one however, you have been the rock in our family, which has held us together all these years. Through all the ups and downs you have always been there for all of us, your unconditional love is instrumental. It was hard hearing you cry the day I broke the news to you, but this is just another hurdle life has thrown our way! Love you mum.

My family, Ian, Paul, Danielle, Janel & Taylah, even though communication is lacking between us all the family bond is strong and knowing I have your support no matter what helps to stay motivated and focused.

Janel, I would like to give a special thanks for your energy and determination to arrange the benefit night held in my honor, the go fund me and your overwhelming level of support. You are a fantastic sister and have always been there no matter what. I don't know where you find the extra time, but I am very grateful for everything you do.

Justin hill, I feel lucky to have you in my corner. From the beginning you have been there helping any way you can, despite dealing with your own challenges. It has meant so much to me and my family in this difficult time, your positivity, and enthusiasm is inspirational. To have you as Giulia's God father is an honor.

Michael Martin, what can I say, your one of a kind, mate! Your uncanny ability to make me laugh out loud has been a godsend. Even when I was at my worst, feeling like the end was drawing near your stories and jokes would bring tears of happiness to my eyes, and being able to laugh in a time like this is irreplaceable. Not to mention all the other ways you have helped me and my family, you know what you have done and can be proud of the person you are, much love brother.

Dylan Francis, we have been through so much growing up, shared a lot of experiences and memories. Even though we have not been in regular contact over the years, every time we catch up, it is like we never left, and this is a testament to your character. Your support throughout this journey has been tremendous and I cannot thank you enough as my words do not do justice for your actions.

Ryan Keith Thomas Johnson, I know there is nothing you would not do for me or my family and knowing this brings me much comfort. You are and have always been a dear friend.

Sean O'Gormlaith & Sammy Breneger, what you both have done for me and my family is unimaginable. I feel undeserving of your actions and can only hope to someday repay you for what you have done, this whole situation would have been a lot different if you were not in my life.

Tarek Ali, I have only met you once or twice and for you to take time out of your personal life and assist with the benefit night was an incredible gesture.

Uncle Johnny, I know I don't need to thank you, but you are an amazing person, your charisma effects all those around you. Your ability to entertain a crowd is second to none and I thank you for your help in the benefit night.

Johnny Lewis, Ella Boot, thank you for taking time out of your busy schedule to attend the benefit night, you both are an inspiration and motivate me to stand up and fight.

Frank Scarfone, you were like a brother growing up, and in this time of need you have shown just how great a mate you are.

Clint Halden, if only we had our chat 10 years ago about the financial strategy! Since we had our beer in April 2019, I have been able to change our situation for good (in this shit time) and focus on something other than my diagnosis / prognosis, which in itself has been a blessing. All I need now is time! Which unfortunately money cannot buy.

Courtney Noble, I found out the hard way what it means to make the wrong decisions when it comes to protecting your wealth. Thanks to you we have been able to navigate the muddy field of insurances and can now rest easy that my wife and I are covered and that our daughter will benefit in such an event. We can put our mind at ease and concentrate our energy towards other areas of our lives now.

Michelle Worthington, I cannot thank you enough, you have helped turn this book idea into reality. Your professionalism and willingness to help in this situation is incredible. Thanks to you this dream has become a reality and because of this we could touch many more lives which is an extraordinary feeling and one which has great satisfaction.

I would like to also take this opportunity to thank those who helped with the benefit night with either supplying items for auction, who took their time out to attend and / or donate money. It was a hard decision to make, to allow my family and friends to arrange such a night. I was taken back by the love and support we have received, and this is another reason I will continue to fight and stay positive no matter how bad things may seem.

CPSIA information can be obtained
at www.ICGtesting.com
Printed in the USA
LVHW061426210620
658102LV00013B/472